MICHAEL OSIRIS SNUFFIN
Introduction to Romantic Satanism

Contents

Introduction

Romantic Satanism was a literary phenomenon that reconstructed and reinterpreted the mythology of Satan, giving him positive attributes and casting him as a heroic rebel against tyranny, oppression, and injustice. The genre was influential between the late 18th and mid-19th centuries. It coincided with the Age of Revolution in Europe (1774-1849) and thus has a distinct revolutionary flavor.

Romantic Satanism is important to modern Satanists and those engaged in Satanic activism for two reasons.

First, Romantic Satanism served as a bridge between the original Christian concept of Satan that was dominant in Europe through the Middle Ages and the modern religious Satanism that emerged in the late 20th century. The Romantic Satanists gave us the first positive portrayals of Satan, and promoted Satanic ideals and concepts now used by modern Satanists. Romantic Satanism has played an important role in the history of Satanism, one that should be recognized and understood.

Second, many of the Romantic Satanists recast Satan as a noble figure struggling against the oppression and tyranny of Church and State. Modern Satanic activists have started using these same Satanic archetypes. Satanic activism has much more in common with the Romantic Satanists of the 19th century than with the social Darwinism of LaVeyan Satanism and its offshoots in the late 20th century.

The primer presents a basic overview of Romantic Satanism, particularly for modern Satanists. Much of the current literature related to Romantic Satanism is geared toward an academic audience. This book aspires to offer an overview of the subject that does not require a degree in Literature or European History.

This examination of Romantic Satanism is divided into five chapters. The first chapter briefly discusses the historical events that changed attitudes about Satan and led to the manifestation of Romantic Satanism. Chapter two examines Romanticism and the themes and theology of Romantic Satanism. Chapter three looks at John Milton and some of the other authors that influenced the first Romantic Satanists. Chapter four analyzes the works of three English Romantic poets that contributed to the Romantic vision of Satan, William Blake, Percy Bysshe Shelley, and Lord Byron. Chapter five examines the French Romantic authors that published works in the genre of Romantic Satanism such as George Sand, Charles Baudelaire, Victor Hugo, and Anatole France.

Understand that none of the authors we will be discussing here were religious Satanists in any way, nor did they identify themselves as Satanists. Many of them used Satan as a literary and/or political metaphor when it suited them and then moved on to other metaphors. Yet it was their vision of Satan as role-model, revolutionary, and hero that paved the way for 20th century religious Satanism.

Chapter One:
Changing Attitudes About Satan

The concept of Satanism is an invention of Christianity. ...it was within the context of Christian religion and of a society shaped by Christian religion that the idea of Satanism first arose. In the big picture, moreover, the emergence of Satanism is fundamentally linked to Christianity by the pivotal role that the latter played in the proliferation of the concept of the devil.[1]

The concept of Satan was integrated into Christian theology around the 4th century. Satan became the embodiment of absolute evil, a force almost as powerful as the God he opposes and a scapegoat for all of the bad things that happened to people. Satan was the serpent that orchestrated the Fall of humanity, turning the earth into a spiritual battleground where God and Satan fought over the human souls. Satan was also the ruler of Hell, the fiery realm of eternal damnation where sinners went when they died. Only by obedience to the Church and the Church-approved State did one escape the clutches of Satan and ascend into Heaven. These ideas persisted for hundreds of years in Europe.

---

[1] Ruben van Lujik, *Children of Lucifer* (New York, Oxford University Press, 2016), 16.

During this time, public accusations of devil worship and witchcraft had serious consequences. Those deemed to be in league with the Devil were imprisoned and tortured, exiled, or killed. During the European Witch Craze (14th-17th century) the Church executed hundreds of thousands of people who were suspected of witchcraft, mostly women. Accusing Jews of being sorcerers and devil-worshipers was popular in the Middle Ages because after the offenders were imprisoned or exiled, their goods and property could be seized. In this climate, anyone willfully identifying with Satanism or authoring positive and sympathetic portrayals of Satan would certainly face a death sentence.

And yet, this is exactly what the first authors of Romantic Satanism accomplished in the late 18th and early 19th centuries. While some risked fines, imprisonment, and/or exile, these authors generally thrived in the Age of Revolution. The first section of this book will explore the historical events and movements that influenced the genre of Romantic Satanism and allowed it to emerge without anyone getting burned at the stake.

The Reformation and Enlightenment

The change started with the Reformation and the Counter-Reformation in the 16th century. Confronted with two competing versions of Christianity, European Christians were forced to re-examine long-held beliefs to determine if they were Catholic or Protestant. New theological concepts and new ways to worship broadened Christian theology. The brutal and destructive wars between European Catholics and Protestants that followed the Reformation fostered an aversion to religion, which became viewed by some as a source of conflict rather than community. Appeals for peace and religious tolerance by secular institutions led to more interest in and involvement with them in society.

The Enlightenment (18th century) brought new challenges to the Church and more development of the mythology of Satan. The emphasis on reason and individualism and the rejection of traditional ideas and values led more people to question religious authority and dogma. Most importantly, the Enlightenment separated "the *idea* of evil from the *image* of the devil."[2] The concept of evil started losing its supernatural nature as more people accepted the secular idea that the source of evil was internal (a corruption inherent in human nature) rather than external (caused by Satan and his minions).

The American and French Revolutions

The American Revolution (1775-1883) established the first post-Enlightenment government, a secular democratic republic which promoted equality, freedom of religion, and individual liberty. The new republic inspired and agitated the citizens of European countries still ruled by monarchy and clergy. The Revolution was won with the help of France, whose close proximity to Britain brought the war to Britain's doorstep. Ironically, the great expense of raising and maintaining a superior army and navy was one of the factors that led to the bankruptcy of the French monarchy and to the French Revolution.

When the French Revolution (1789-1799) replaced the monarchy with the First Republic, many people in Europe hoped that the new government would be as stable and equitable as the new American republic. It wasn't.

During the first part of the French Revolution, after the radical Jacobins seized power in the government, the country was quickly and brutally de-Christianized. Priests who would not swear an oath

---

[2]   Stephen E. Flowers, *Lords of the Left-Hand Path* (Rochester, Inner Traditions, 2012), 180.

to the state were exiled or executed, and Church property was sold off. For a very brief time in history, traditionally Catholic France ceased to be a Christian nation.

The Jacobins were also responsible for the Reign of Terror, in which thousands of suspected enemies of the Revolution were executed via the guillotine. The French Revolutionary Wars (1792-1802) forcibly spread the ideals of the Revolution to other regions and countries. The execution of Louis XVI horrified European monarchs and royalists, who called for war against the Revolution. The revolutionary fervor inspired by the initial success of the Revolution in throwing off the yoke of the Old Regime soured when what replaced it turned out to be much worse. Only under the dictatorship of Napoleon did the French government finally stabilize.

Under Napoleon, the Concordant of 1801 reestablished the presence and status of the Catholic Church in France, which helped to mend the breach between revolutionaries and Catholics. However, Napoleon still reserved the right to nominate Bishops (which gave him control over parishes around the country), and Church property sold off during the Revolution was not restored. The Catholic Church never regained the power and influence it had possessed before the Revolution.

During and after the French Revolution, conspiracy theories circulated among anti-revolutionaries alleging that anti-Christian forces were behind the Revolution. Revolutionaries were labeled Satanic or evil by political and religious conservatives. After the Revolution, Napoleon was often compared with the Devil or the Antichrist by conservatives. Many Romantic Satanists used this propaganda to their advantage, casting Satan as a rebel and revolutionary against conservative tyranny. The French Revolution became a popular subject for Romantic Satanists; in a letter to Byron, Shelley described the

Revolution as "the master theme of the epoch in which we live."[3]

The British Reaction

The British government initially welcomed the French Revolution because they believed that it would weaken France's influence in Europe. The British became alarmed when the French Revolutionary Wars and Napoleonic Wars expanded the territory of France and spread the revolution to other countries, especially along the northern coast of Continental Europe. The British allied with other European powers to contain the French empire, and the defeat of Napoleon in 1815 restored the balance of power in Europe.

In 1811, King George III was deemed mentally unfit to rule, so his son stepped in as the King's Regent. The Regency (1811-1820) was a period of great cultural and artistic achievements but also of great poverty and squalor among the underclass. Britain was not immune from the revolutionary fervor inspired by the French Revolution, and calls for societal and political reforms became more frequent. Strikes and protests erupted, sometimes into violence. The Peterloo Massacre in 1819, in which the local militia attacked a crowd of protesters seeking reform and voting rights, provoked horror and outrage around the country that brought further unrest. Fearing an armed rebellion, the British Parliament passed repressive legislation in 1820 known as the Six Acts, allowing magistrates to ban public demonstrations and to search for and seize firearms on private property. They also streamlined the courts to speed up the justice system and increased taxes and restrictions on newspapers.

Most important to the development of Romantic Satanism was the

---

[3] Stephen Greenblatt et al., Eds., *The Norton Anthology of English Literature*, 9th ed., Vol D (*New York, W.W. Norton & Company, 2012*), 183.

Blasphemous and Seditious Libels Act, which increased the penalties for writing and publishing blasphemous and seditious materials. This was the most repressive of recent censorship laws passed in England. The English poets Percy Shelley and Lord Byron, both proponents of political reform, challenged these laws by writing and publishing material with blasphemous and seditious themes, and one of their favorite themes was Satan.

Chapter Two:
Elements of Romantic Satanism

Romanticism and Romantic Satanism

Romanticism was an artistic and intellectual movement influential between the late 18th and mid-19th centuries. It was in part a reaction to the Enlightenment and the Industrial Revolution. It thus valued imagination and emotion over reason, nature over urbanization and mechanization, subjectivity over objectivity, and the supernatural over science. Other aspects of Romanticism include individualism, freedom from conventions, solitary living, spontaneity, the eccentric, and the exotic.

Many of these characteristics were embodied in the Romantic hero, a strong-willed but flawed individual who defied societal laws and conventions, and whose eccentricities and transgressions often isolated them from society. Romantic heroes were intensely introspective, and thus authors often emphasized their thoughts and emotions over their actions. Romantic heroes may have lacked heroic qualities, yet they often behaved in a heroic manner. The Satanic hero and the Byronic hero were darker variants of the Romantic hero.[4]

Another important concept of Romanticism was that of the sublime. Philosopher Edmund Burke described the sublime as "whatever is fitted in any sort to excite the ideas of pain and danger, that is to say, whatever is in any sort terrible, or is conversant about terrible objects, or operates in a manner analogous to terror, is a source of the sublime; that is, it is productive of the strongest emotion which the mind is capable of feeling."[5]

The sublime is often experienced in nature; the grandeur of snow-covered mountains, the towering trees of old forests, and the immensity of the ocean that stretches to the horizon all evoke sublime feelings. Romantic writers sought to evoke these intense feelings in poem and prose.

Burke continues:

> *The passion caused by the great and sublime in nature, when those causes operate most powerfully, is astonishment; and astonishment is that state of the soul, in which all its motions are suspended, with some degree of horror. In this case the mind is so entirely filled with its object, that it cannot entertain any other, nor by consequence reason on that object which employs it. Hence arises the great power of the sublime, that, far from being produced by them, it anticipates our reasonings, and hurries us on by an irresistible force. Astonishment, as I have said, is the effect of the sublime in*

---

[4] Romantic heroes within the genre of Romantic Satanism include Cythna from Shelley's *Revolt of Islam* and Prometheus in Shelley's *Prometheus Unbound*; the titular characters in Byron's *Manfred* and *Cain*; and Arcade from France's *Revolt of the Angels*.

[5] Edmund Burke, *A Philosophical Inquiry into the Origin of Our Ideas on the Sublime and Beautiful*, Part 1, Chapter 7: "Of the Sublime," in Charles W. Eliot, Ed., *The Harvard Classics Shelf of Fiction* (New York, P.F. Collier & Son, 1917), https://www.bartleby.com/24/2/.

its highest degree; the inferior effects are admiration, reverence, and respect.[6]

The term Romantic Satanism describes Romantic literature that focuses on Satan or Satanic themes. Many authors within this genre regarded John Milton's Satan from *Paradise Lost* as a sublime figure, a mythical, larger-than-life antihero rebelling against an overwhelming and omnipotent oppressor:

> *In an inversion of traditional (and more conventional contemporary) usages of Satan as the moving power behind the enemy, he became a symbol for the struggle against tyranny, injustice, and oppression. He was made into a mythical figure of rebellion for an age of revolutions, a larger-than-life individual for an age of individualism, a free thinker in an age struggling for free thought.*[7]

Themes of Romantic Satanism

There are five common themes found in the genre of Romantic Satanism: **Reinterpretation, Inversion, Revolution, Redemption,** and **Normalization**. Most of the works we will examine will have two or three of these themes.

1. **Reinterpretation.** The author presents a positive re-evaluation of Biblical or Satanic mythology. One of the most common subjects of **reinterpretation** is the Biblical mythology surrounding the serpent of Genesis, traditionally representative of Satan. Disconnecting the

---

[6] Burke, *On the Sublime and Beautiful.* Part 2, Chapter 1: "Of the Passion Caused by the Sublime."

[7] Asbjørn Dyrendal, James R. Lewis, and Jesper AA. Petersen, *The Invention of Satanism* (New York, Oxford University Press, 2016), 30-31.

serpent from Satan means that Satan is not responsible for the Fall of Humanity or original sin. In the Gnostic reinterpretation of the myth, the world is created by an evil demiurge, and the Satan-serpent saves humanity from a life of eternal ignorance. These Biblical and Gnostic **reinterpretations** invalidate the concept of original sin, which in turn negates the need for salvation through Christ.

2. **Inversion.** The author inverts the traditional associations of God and Satan with good and evil, where Satan is considered good, and God evil. **Inversion** is usually employed with little or no explanation.

3. **Revolution.** The author portrays Satan as an archetypal rebel against God's oppressive authority, a revolutionary hero, and/or a symbol of liberty. This theme was inspired by the Romantic re-evaluation of Milton and informed by the Age of Revolution.

4. **Redemption.** The author orchestrates the redemption or reconciliation of Satan with God and/or Jesus to bring about the Second Coming and/or a utopian civilization. Bringing Satan and God together ends the war between Heaven and Hell and ushers in a new post-Christian utopian civilization.

5. **Normalization.** The author normalizes Satan by giving him a human appearance and emotions, or by depicting Satan interacting with people in normal society. **Normalization** usually makes it easier for people to sympathize with or understand Satan.

Theology of Romantic Satanism

The Romantic Satanists used certain theological concepts in their literature that may not be familiar to all readers. Some of these concepts come from the Bible, while others predate Christianity.

The Biblical Creation and the Fall of Humanity—The second and third chapters of Genesis in the Old Testament describe the creation of the Garden of Eden and of man and woman. The new couple are warned not to eat from one tree in the middle of the garden, the tree of knowledge of good and evil; if they do, they will perish. A serpent tempts Eve to eat from the forbidden tree, telling her that the fruit will not kill them but will open their eyes and make them like gods, giving them knowledge of good and evil. Eve and then Adam eat fruit from the tree and are awakened. God finds out, curses them, and banishes them from the Garden of Eden. Their disobedience became the source of the concept of original sin, the state of sin that everyone is born into, the hereditary curse of all descendants of Adam and Eve.

For over a thousand years the serpent from this myth was firmly connected with Satan, making Satan responsible for the Fall of Humanity and the existence of sin in the world. However, this connection is not mentioned in the Bible, and Christian deconstructionists in the 18th century used this fact to disconnect Satan from the serpent in their efforts to discredit both the creation myth of the Bible and the concept of original sin.

The Fall of the Angels—This concept originates in the Book of Revelation 12:7-9:

> *Then war broke out in heaven; Michael and his angels battled against the dragon. The dragon and its angels fought back, but they did not prevail and there was no longer any place for them in heaven. The huge dragon, the ancient serpent, who is called the Devil and Satan, who deceived the whole world, was thrown down to earth, and its angels were thrown down with it.*[8]

Parallels are often made to Isaiah 14:12:

> *How you have fallen from the heavens, O Morning Star, son of*

---

[8] All Bible quotes are taken from the New American Bible, Revised Edition (NABRE).

the dawn! How you have been cut down to the earth, you who conquered nations!

Lucifer is the name of the Morning Star; this is where the Biblical connection between Lucifer and Satan is established.

Zoroastrianism—This ancient Persian religion based on the teachings of Zoroaster (aka Zarathustra) dates back to the 6th century BCE. Considered by some to be the first monotheistic faith, it is one of the oldest continuously practiced religions in the world. Zoroastrians believe in Ahura Mazda, the supreme creator, who is opposed by and will eventually prevail over the destructive spirit Angra Mainyu. Zoroastrianism influenced both Judaism and Christianity, religions that adapted Zoroastrian concepts such as monotheism, Heaven and Hell, and a day of judgment.

Gnosticism—This religious movement started in the first and second centuries. Gnosticism emphasizes salvation through personal spiritual knowledge (or *gnosis*) of the supreme deity rather than through faith. The Gnostics believed that the world was created and ruled by an evil demiurge, who trapped the divine spark within matter; thus there is a divine spark trapped within each of us. Gnostics see the material world as evil, as the source of pain and suffering; one can overcome this state by cultivating the divine spark within and releasing it from its material prison.

In Gnostic Christianity, the Fall of Humanity takes on a different meaning. The evil demiurge traps Adam and Eve in a state of ignorance within the Garden of Eden. The serpent is the messiah who encourages the first couple to eat from the tree of knowledge, which lifts them out of ignorance and frees them from slavery.

Manichaeism—Founded by the Persian prophet Mani in the latter half of the third century, this dualistic religious system was a synthesis of Christian, Gnostic, and Pagan beliefs; it was also influenced by

Zoroastrianism. Manichaeism describes the nature of the universe as a struggle between the spiritual world of light and the material world of darkness.

Chapter Three:
Milton's Rise and the Devil's Demise

Milton's *Paradise Lost* was the touchstone for Romantic Satanism. This chapter examines Milton's Satan and the popular reinterpretations that followed. It also includes examples of the deconstruction of traditional Satanic mythology that influenced the first Romantic Satanists.

John Milton: Paradise Lost

English poet, essayist, and civil servant John Milton (1608-1674) is considered to be one of the greatest English poets. He studied for the priesthood at Christ's College, Cambridge, but never became a priest. Milton was well-read and well-traveled, and he was politically active against the monarchy in the English Civil War (1642-1651).

Milton's *Paradise Lost* explores the biblical story of the Fall of humanity, beginning with the war in Heaven, where Satan is cast down to Hell, and ending with the fall of Adam and Eve. *Paradise Lost* was first published in 1667; a revised edition was published in 1674, the year of Milton's death. Milton's purpose is stated at the beginning of the poem:

> —*What in me is dark,*
> *Illumin; what is low raise and support;*

That to the highth of this great Argument,
I may assert Eternal Providence,
And justifie the wayes of God to men.[9]

Milton's poem humanized Satan, who is portrayed at the beginning of the poem as a fallen angel, not the bestial man-goat hybrid of the Middle Ages or the grotesque monster at the center of Dante's *Inferno*. Milton gives Satan human feelings, doubts, and aspirations.

Is this the Region, this the Soil, the Clime,
Said then the lost Arch-Angel, this the seat
That we must change for Heav'n, this mournful gloom
For that celestial light? Be it so, since he
Who now is Sovran can dispose and bid
What shall be right: fardest from him is best
Whom reason hath equald, force hath made supream
Above his equals. Farewel happy Fields
Where Joy for ever dwells: Hail horrours, hail
Infernal world, and thou profoundest Hell
Receive thy new Possessor: One who brings
A mind not to be chang'd by Place or Time.
The mind is its own place, and in it self
Can make a Heav'n of Hell, a Hell of Heav'n.
What matter where, if I be still the same,
And what I should be, all but less then he
Whom Thunder hath made greater? Here at least
We shall be free; th' Almighty hath not built
Here for his envy, will not drive us hence:

---

[9] John Milton, *Paradise Lost*, Book 1, lines 22-26, https://www.dartmouth.edu/~milton/reading_room/pl/book_1/text.shtml.

Here we may reign secure, and in my choyce
To reign is worth ambition though in Hell:
Better to reign in Hell, then serve in Heav'n.[10]

Later, Satan gives a heroic speech to roust the fallen angels:

He call'd so loud, that all the hollow Deep
Of Hell resounded. Princes, Potentates,
Warriers, the Flowr of Heav'n, once yours, now lost,
If such astonishment as this can sieze
Eternal spirits; or have ye chos'n this place
After the toyl of Battel to repose
Your wearied vertue, for the ease you find
To slumber here, as in the Vales of Heav'n?
Or in this abject posture have ye sworn
To adore the Conquerour? who now beholds
Cherube and Seraph rowling in the Flood
With scatter'd Arms and Ensigns, till anon
His swift pursuers from Heav'n Gates discern
Th' advantage, and descending tread us down
Thus drooping, or with linked Thunderbolts
Transfix us to the bottom of this Gulfe.
Awake, arise, or be for ever fall'n.
They heard, and were abasht, and up they sprung[11]

Paradise Lost became popular reading in the 18th century, and it also served as the foundation for Romantic Satanism. To the first wave of authors of works of Romantic Satanism, few things were more sublime

---

[10] Milton, *Paradise Lost*, Book 1, lines 242-263.

[11] Ibid, lines 314-331.

than Milton's epic *Paradise Lost*. They quoted from it, made allusions to it in poetry, and praised it in prose.

Edmund Burke: On the Sublime and Beautiful

Irish politician and philosopher Edmund Burke (1730-1797) wrote one of the landmarks of English romanticism, *A Philosophical Enquiry into the Origin of Our Ideas of the Sublime and Beautiful* (1757), 70 years after the publication of *Paradise Lost*. He was one of the first popular authors to reinterpret Milton's Satan in a positive light:

> *The ideas of eternity, and infinity, are among the most affecting we have: and yet perhaps there is nothing of which we really understand so little, as of infinity and eternity. We do not anywhere meet a more sublime description than this justly-celebrated one of Milton, wherein he gives the portrait of Satan with a dignity so suitable to the subject:*
>
> *"—He above the rest*
> *In shape and gesture proudly eminent*
> *Stood like a tower; his form had yet not lost*
> *All her original brightness, nor appeared*
> *Less than archangel ruined, and the excess*
> *Of glory obscured: as when the sun new risen*
> *Looks through the horizontal misty air*
> *Shorn of his beams; or from behind the moon*
> *In dim eclipse disastrous twilight sheds*
> *On half the nations; and with fear of change*
> *Perplexes monarchs."*[12]
>
> *Here is a very noble picture; and in what does this poetical picture*

---

[12] Ibid, lines 589-599.

consist? In images of a tower, an archangel, the sun rising through mists, or in an eclipse, the ruin of monarchs, and the revolutions of kingdoms. The mind is hurried out of itself, by a crowd of great and confused images; which affect because they are crowded and confused. For, separate them, and you lose much of the greatness; and join them, and you infallibly lose the clearness.[13]

Burke also wrote *Reflections on the Revolution in France* (1790), an intellectual attack on the French Revolution. While some academics claim that Burke repeatedly connected French revolutionaries with Satan in his *Reflections*,[14] an examination of the text reveals no overt references.

William Godwin: An Enquiry into Political Justice

The first Romantic Satanists were influenced by Joseph Johnson (1738-1809), an influential and successful publisher and bookseller in 18th century London. Johnson hosted regular dinners for influential poets, artists, and authors, attracting a loose group of political radicals that became known as the Johnson Circle. Johnson wanted to produce and publish a new illustrated version of Milton's epic poem, which had become popular in the 18th century. His project failed to materialize, but his efforts inspired members of the Johnson Circle to explore Milton's conception of Satan.

English author and philosopher William Godwin (1756-1836) was

---

[13] Burke, *On the Sublime and Beautiful*, Part II, Chapter 4: "Of the Difference Between Clearness and Obscurity with Regard to the Passions."

[14] Peter A. Schock, *Romantic Satanism: Myth and the Historical Movement in Blake, Shelley, and Byron* (Houndmills, UK, Palgrave Macmillan, 2003), 21; Per Faxneld, *Satanic Feminism: Lucifer as the Liberator of Woman in Nineteenth-Century Culture* (New York, Oxford University Press, 2017), 75.

one of the radicals drawn to Johnson's table. His works attacked political institutions and advocated the philosophies of utilitarianism and anarchism. Godwin met his future wife, the feminist author Mary Wollstonecraft, at one of the Johnson Circle dinners.

In what many regard as Godwin's most important and influential work, *An Enquiry into Political Justice* (1793), he explores the character of Milton's Satan:

> *It has no doubt resulted from a train of speculation similar to this, that poetical readers have commonly remarked Milton's devil to be a being of considerable virtue. It must be admitted that his energies centred too much in personal regards. But why did he rebel against his maker? It was, as he himself informs us, because he saw no sufficient reason for that extreme inequality of rank and power which the creator assumed. It was because prescription and precedent form no adequate ground for implicit faith. After his fall, why did he still cherish the spirit of opposition? From a persuasion that he was hardly and injuriously treated. He was not discouraged by the apparent inequality of the contest: because a sense of reason and justice was stronger in his mind than a sense of brute force; because he had much of the feelings of an Epictetus or a Cato, and little of those of a slave. He bore his torments with fortitude, because he disdained to be subdued by despotic power. He sought revenge, because he could not think with tameness of the unexpostulating authority that assumed to dispose of him. How beneficial and illustrious might the temper from which these qualities flowed have been found, with a small diversity of situation!*[15]

---

[15] William Godwin, *An Enquiry into Political Justice, and its Influence on General Virtue and Happiness, Vol. 1*, Book IV, Chapter IV, Appendix No. 1 (London, G.G.J. and J. Robinson, 1793). https://oll.libertyfund.org/titles/godwin-an-enquiry-concerning-political-justice-vol-i.

Peter Schock remarks that "it was the idealization of Satan in *Political Justice* that first established this mythic figure as an icon of insurrection."[16] Shelley was so impressed with Godwin's *Political Justice* and other works that he visited him in 1814.

Voltaire: Philosophical Dictionary

While some authors were constructing a positive perspective of Milton's Satan, other authors were deconstructing the Christian mythology surrounding Satan.

The French philosopher and author Voltaire (1694-1778) was a deist well-known for his attacks on the religious and political establishment. He was an Enlightenment advocate for freedom of speech, religious tolerance, and the separation of church and state, and he was imprisoned twice and exiled for many years for his critiques of the French government. Voltaire's magnum opus, the satiric novella *Candide*, was banned after publication due to its scathing satire of the church and the government.

Voltaire's *Philosophical Dictionary* (1764) was a series of radical essays that are often critical of religion, particularly the Catholic Church. His entry on *Angels* reveals that the Jews and Christians took their ideas of angels and devils from other religions and cultures:

> *The doctrine of angels is one of the oldest in the world. It preceded that of the immortality of the soul. This is not surprising; philosophy is necessary to the belief that the soul of mortal man is immortal; but imagination and weakness are sufficient for the invention of beings superior to ourselves, protecting or persecuting us. Yet it does not appear that the ancient Egyptians had any*

---

[16] Schock, *Romantic Satanism*, 115.

notion of these celestial beings, clothed with an ethereal body and administering to the orders of a God. The ancient Babylonians were the first who admitted this theology. The Hebrew books employ the angels from the first book of Genesis downwards: but the Book of Genesis was not written before the Chaldeans had become a powerful nation: nor was it until the captivity of Babylon that the Jews learned the names of Gabriel, Raphael, Michael, Uriel, etc., which were given to the angels. The Jewish and Christian religions being founded on the fall of Adam, and this fall being founded on the temptation by the evil angel, the devil, it is very singular that not a word is said in the Pentateuch of the existence of the bad angels, still less of their punishment and abode in hell.

The reason of this omission is evident: the evil angels were unknown to the Jews until the Babylonian captivity; then it is that Asmodeus begins to be talked of, whom Raphael went to bind in Upper Egypt; there it is that the Jews first hear of Satan. This word Satan was Chaldean; and the Book of Job, an inhabitant of Chaldea, is the first that makes mention of him. [17]

Voltaire was also critical of the fall of the angels:

The story of the fall of the angels is not to be found in the books of Moses. The first testimony respecting it is that of Isaiah, who, apostrophizing the king of Babylon, exclaims, "Where is now the exacter of tributes? The pines and the cedars rejoice in his fall. How hast thou fallen from heaven, O Hellel, star of the morning?" It has been already observed that the word Hellel has been rendered

---

[17] Voltaire, *The Philosophical Dictionary*, H.I. Woolf, ed. (New York, Knopf, 1924), Chapter 29, "Angels," https://history.hanover.edu/texts/voltaire/volindex.htm.

by the Latin word Lucifer; that afterwards, in an allegorical sense, the name of Lucifer was given to the prince of the angels, who made war in heaven; and that, at last, this word, signifying Phosphorus and Aurora, *has become the name of the devil.*

The Christian religion is founded on the fall of the angels. Those who revolted were precipitated from the spheres which they inhabited into hell, in the centre of the earth, and became devils. A devil, in the form of a serpent, tempted Eve, and damned mankind. Jesus came to redeem mankind, and to triumph over the devil, who tempts us still. Yet this fundamental tradition is to be found nowhere but in the apocryphal book of Enoch; and there it is in a form quite different from that of the received tradition."[18]

In his entry on *Genesis*, Voltaire deconstructed the story of the Garden of Eden:

"Eat not of the fruit of the tree of knowledge of good and evil." It is not easy to conceive that there ever existed a tree which could teach good and evil, as there are trees that bear pears and apricots. And besides the question is asked, why is God unwilling that man should know good and evil? Would not his free access to this knowledge, on the contrary, appear — if we may venture to use such language — more worthy of God, and far more necessary to man? To our weak reason it would seem more natural and proper for God to command him to eat largely of such fruit; but we must bring our reason under subjection, and acquiesce with humility and simplicity in the conclusion that God is to be obeyed.

"If thou shalt eat thereof, thou shalt die." Nevertheless, Adam ate of it and did not die; on the contrary, he is stated to have lived on

---

[18] Voltaire, *The Philosophical Dictionary*, Chapter 29, Angels

for nine hundred and thirty years. Many of the fathers considered the whole matter as an allegory. In fact, it might be said that all other animals have no knowledge that they shall die, but that man, by means of his reason, has such knowledge. This reason is the tree of knowledge which enables him to foresee his end. This, perhaps, is the most rational interpretation that can be given. We venture not to decide positively.[19]

And as for the serpent:

"But the serpent was more subtle than all animals on the earth; he said to the woman," etc. Throughout the whole of this article there is no mention made of the devil. Everything in it relates to the usual course of nature. The serpent was considered by all oriental nations, not only as the most cunning of all animals, but likewise as immortal. The Chaldeans had a fable concerning a quarrel between God and the serpent, and this fable had been preserved by Pherecydes. Origen cites it in his sixth book against Celsus. A serpent was borne in procession at the feasts of Bacchus. The Egyptians, according to the statement of Eusebius in the first book of the tenth chapter of his "Evangelical Preparation," attached a sort of divinity to the serpent. In Arabia, India, and even China, the serpent was regarded as a symbol of life; and hence it was that the emperors of China, long before the time of Moses, always bore upon their breast the image of a serpent.[20]

The anonymously published *Philosophical Dictionary* was popular with the masses but it offended religious authorities and was censored by

---

[19] Voltaire, *Philosophical Dictionary*, Chapter 232, Genesis.

[20] Ibid.

the French government.

Thomas Paine: The Age of Reason

Thomas Paine (1737-1809) was born in England; after many unsuccessful careers and two failed marriages, Paine relocated to Philadelphia at the end of 1774 with the help of Ben Franklin. Paine published the pamphlet *Common Sense* (1776), which advocated complete independence from the British and influenced the Declaration of Independence. Paine also fought in the revolutionary army and was involved with new government for a short time.

In 1787 Paine went to England to raise funds for a bridge project. He got caught up in the events of the French Revolution and moved to France in 1790. Edmund Burke's criticism of the Revolution in *Reflections on the Revolution in France* (1790) prompted Paine and other pro-Revolution notables to respond. Paine wrote *Rights of Man* (1791) and *Rights of Man, Part II* (1792), defending not only the French Revolution but also advocating for political reform in England, where he was indicted and convicted *in absentia* for seditious libel.

He was initially welcomed by the new French Government but was later jailed and almost executed during the Reign of Terror. During this time Paine worked on *The Age of Reason*, which was published in three parts in 1794, 1795, and 1807. Subtitled An *Investigation of True and Fabulous Theology*, his work advocated Deism, attacked orthodox Christianity, and questioned the legitimacy of the Bible.

Paine's deconstruction of Satanic mythology is based on a strictly literal interpretation of the Bible:

> *The Christian Mythologists, after having confined Satan in a pit,*
> *were obliged to let him out again to bring on the sequel of the fable.*
> *He is then introduced into the Garden of Eden, in the shape of*

a snake or a serpent, and in that shape he enters into familiar conversation with Eve, who is no way surprised to hear a snake talk; and the issue of this tête-à-tête is that he persuades her to eat an apple, and the eating of that apple damns all mankind.

After giving Satan this triumph over the whole creation, one would have supposed that the Church Mythologists would have been kind enough to send him back again to the pit; ... . But instead of this they leave him at large, without even obliging him to give his parole—the secret of which is, that they could not do without him; and after being at the trouble of making him, they bribed him to stay. They promised him ALL the Jews, ALL the Turks by anticipation, nine-tenths of the world beside, and Mahomet into the bargain. After this, who can doubt the bountifulness of the Christian Mythology?

Having thus made an insurrection and a battle in Heaven, in which none of the combatants could be either killed or wounded—put Satan into the pit—let him out again—giving him a triumph over the whole creation—damned all mankind by the eating of an apple, these Christian Mythologists bring the two ends of their fable together. They represent this virtuous and amiable man, Jesus Christ, to be at once both God and Man, and also the Son of God, celestially begotten, on purpose to be sacrificed, because they say that Eve in her longing had eaten an apple.[21]

Paine then exposes how the "Christian Mythologists" ironically give Satan almost unlimited power over the Earth:

---

[21] Thomas Paine, *Age of Reason,* Part First, Sections 2-3, https://web.archive.org/web/20050306021320/http://www.ushistory.org/-paine/reason/index.htm.

In order to make for it a foundation to rise upon, the inventors were under the necessity of giving to the being whom they call Satan, a power equally as great, if not greater than they attribute to the Almighty. They have not only given him the power of liberating himself from the pit, after what they call his fall, but they have made that power increase afterward to infinity. Before this fall they represent him only as an angel of limited existence, as they represent the rest. After his fall, he becomes, by their account, omnipresent. He exists everywhere, and at the same time. He occupies the whole immensity of space.

Not content with this deification of Satan, they represent him as defeating, by stratagem, in the shape of an animal of the creation, all the power and wisdom of the Almighty. They represent him as having compelled the Almighty to the direct necessity either of surrendering the whole of the creation to the government and sovereignty of this Satan, or of capitulating for its redemption by coming down upon earth, and exhibiting himself upon a cross in the shape of a man.

Had the inventors of this story told it the contrary way, that is, had they represented the Almighty as compelling Satan to exhibit himself on a cross, in the shape of a snake, as a punishment for his new transgression, the story would have been less absurd—less contradictory. But instead of this, they make the transgressor triumph, and the Almighty fall.[22]

Paine concludes that "...it is impossible to conceive a story more derogatory to the Almighty, more inconsistent with his wisdom, more contradictory to his power, than this story is."

The Age of Reason had little impact in revolutionary France, but it

---

[22] Paine, *Age of Reason*, Part First, Sections 2-3

sparked outrage in back in England, where radical publisher Daniel Isaac Eaton was tried and convicted of blasphemous libel in 1812 for publishing Paine's book. As we will see, increasingly restrictive blasphemy laws in England were of great concern to the first Romantic Satanists.

Chapter Four:
The English Romantic Satanists

William Blake: The Marriage of Heaven and Hell

English poet and artist William Blake (1757-1827) was the first major author to write in the genre of Romantic Satanism. He was a member of the Johnson Circle, and Johnson commissioned Blake to illustrate a number of works, including his *Paradise Lost* project. Blake wrote and illustrated a few works loosely influenced by *Paradise Lost*, including the poem *Milton* (1805-08). He was working on a series of engravings for an edition of Dante's *Divine Comedy* when he died.

Blake is considered to be one of the greatest English poets. He is also renowned for his engravings and illustrations, which included scenes from Dante's *Inferno*, *Paradise Lost*, and the Bible; thus Satan was a frequent subject. Blake was Christian but opposed both Deism and Orthodox Christianity. He believed Jesus to be a gifted prophet, but not the son of God. Blake also had spiritual visions throughout his life that inspired many of his works, especially *America: A Prophecy* (1793) and *Europe: A Prophecy* (1794).

William Blake's greatest contribution to Romantic Satanism was the iconoclastic work *The Marriage of Heaven and Hell* (ca.1790). There are Satanic themes in most of William Blake's subsequent works;

unfortunately, they revolve around a personal and nebulous pantheon of ever-changing deities, with the Satanic mantle passed between them in an almost haphazard fashion, and we will not examine them here.

The Marriage of Heaven and Hell is a collection of poems, stories, observations, and criticism regarding religious and spiritual matters. The work was in part a response to *Heaven and Hell* (1758), a book published in Latin by Swedish scientist and mystic Emanuel Swedenborg. *Heaven and Hell* was a text Swedenborg claimed to have received from God that described the afterlife, including Heaven, Hell, and the spirit world. Blake had been interested in Swedenborg's theology in the early 1780's, but by the end of the decade Blake had only ridicule and scorn for Swedenborg:

> *I have always found that Angels have the vanity to speak of themselves as the only wise; this they do with a confident insolence sprouting from systematic reasoning;*
>
> *Thus Swedenborg boasts that what he writes is new; tho' it is only the Contents or Index of already publish'd books*
>
> *A man carried a monkey about for a shew, & because he was a little wiser than the monkey, grew vain, and conceiv'd himself as much wiser than seven men. It is so with Swedenborg: he shows the folly of churches and exposes hypocrites, till he imagines that all are religious. & himself the single one on earth that ever broke a net.*
>
> *Now hear a plain fact: Swedenborg has not written one new truth: Now hear another: he has written all the old falsehoods.*
>
> *And now hear the reason. He conversed with Angels who are all religious, & conversed not with Devils who all hate religion, for he was incapable thro' his conceited notions.*
>
> *Thus Swedenborgs writings are a recapitulation of all superficial*

opinions, and an analysis of the more sublime, but no further.[23]

The first part of *The Marriage of Heaven and Hell* describes an **inversion** of good and evil forces symbolized by Heaven and Hell, a theme that permeates Blake's "Bible of Hell":

Without Contraries is no progression. Attraction and Repulsion, Reason and Energy, Love and Hate, are necessary to Human existence.

From these contraries spring what the religious call Good & Evil. Good is the passive that obeys Reason

Evil is the active springing from Energy.

Good is Heaven. Evil is Hell.

The voice of the Devil

All Bibles or sacred codes. have been the causes of the following Errors.

1. That Man has two real existing principles Viz: a Body & a Soul.

2. That Energy. called Evil. is alone from the Body. & that Reason. called Good. is alone from the Soul.

3. That God will torment Man in Eternity for following his Energies.

But the following Contraries to these are True

1. Man has no Body distinct from his Soul for that called Body is a portion of Soul discernd by the five Senses, the chief inlets of Soul in this age.

---

[23] William Blake, *The Poetical Works of William Blake*, John Sampson, Ed. (New York, Oxford University Press, 1908), https://www.bartleby.com/235/253.html. I have preserved Blake's unusual punctuation and formatting.

> *2, Energy is the only life and is from the Body and Reason is the*
> *bound or outward circumference of Energy.*
> *3. Energy is Eternal Delight*[24]

Blake's correction of perceived errors in sacred texts leads to an association between evil, energy, life and eternal delight. Like a good Romantic writer, Blake elevates energy (emotion and passion) above reason, and exercising this energy leads to eternal delight, not eternal torment. In essence, he denies the concept of sin.

Blake also condemns the priesthood as oppressors of the "vulgar":

> *The ancient Poets animated all sensible objects with Gods or*
> *Geniuses, calling them by the names and adorning them with*
> *the properties of woods, rivers, mountains, lakes, cities, nations,*
> *and whatever their enlarged & numerous senses could perceive.*
>
> *And particularly they studied the genius of each city & country,*
> *placing it under its mental deity.*
>
> *Till a system was formed, which some took advantage of &*
> *enslav'd the vulgar by attempting to realize or abstract the mental*
> *deities from their objects; thus began Priesthood.*
>
> *Choosing forms of worship from poetic tales.*
>
> *And at length they pronounced that the gods had orderd such*
> *things.*
>
> *Thus men forgot that All deities reside in the human breast.*[25]

Blake's implies that humanity is the source of all gods, that all deities come from within, and thus priests, as the intermediaries between men and gods, are not necessary for spiritual development.

---

[24] Blake, *Poetical Works.*

[25] Ibid.

Another section of the book lists the "Proverbs of Hell" after this devilish introduction:

> *As I was walking among the fires of hell, delighted with the enjoyments of Genius; which to Angels look like torment and insanity. I collected some of their Proverbs: thinking that as sayings used in a nation, mark its character, so the Proverbs of Hell, shew the nature of Infernal wisdom better than any description of buildings or garments*[26]

Most of the proverbs are practical or philosophical statements, but some are critical of religion:

> *Prisons are built with stones of Law, Brothels with bricks of Religion.*
> *The pride of the peacock is the glory of God.*
> *The lust of the goat is the bounty of God.*
> *The wrath of the lion is the wisdom of God.*
> *The nakedness of woman is the work of God.*

> *As the catterpiller chooses the fairest leaves to layer her eggs on, so the priest lays his curse on the fairest joys.*

> *As the plow follows words, so God rewards prayers.*
> *Prayers plow not! Praises reap not!* [27]

Blake also weighs in on the nature of Hell:

---

[26] Ibid.

[27] Ibid.

An Angel came to me and said O pitiable foolish young man! O horrible! O dreadful state! consider the hot burning dungeon thou art preparing for thyself to all eternity, to which thou art going in such a career.

I said. perhaps you will be willing to shew me my eternal lot & we will contemplate together upon it and see whether your lot or mine is most desirable

So he took me thro' a stable & thro' a church & down into the church vault at the end of which was a mill; thro' the mill we went, and came to a cave. down the winding cavern we groped our tedious way till a void boundless as a nether sky appeared us, & we held by the roots of trees and hung over this immensity, but I said, if you please we will commit ourselves to this void, and see whether this providence is here also, if you will not I will? but he answer, do not presume O young man but as we here remain behold thy lot which will soon appear when the darkness passes away.

So I remained with him sitting in the twisted root of an oak, he was suspended in a fungus which hung with the head downward into the deep:

By degrees we beheld the infinite Abyss, fiery as the smoke of a burning city; beneath us at an immense distance was the sun, black but shining round it were fiery tracks on which revolv'd vast spiders, crawling after their prey; which flew or rather swum in infinite deep, in the most terrific shapes of animals sprung from corruption. & the air was full of them, & seemd composed of them; these are Devils. and are called Powers of the air, I now asked my companion which was my eternal lot? he said, between the black & white spiders

But now, from between the black & white spiders a cloud and fire burst and rolled thro the deep blackning all beneath, so that the nether deep grew black as a sea & rolled with a terrible noise:

beneath us was nothing now to be seen but a black tempest, till looking east between the clouds & the waves. we saw a cataract of blood mixed with fire and not many stones throw from us appeard and sunk again the scaly fold of a monstrous serpent. at last to the east, distant about three degrees appeard a fiery crest above the waves slowly it reared like a ridge of golden rocks till we discoverd two globes of crimson fire. from which the sea fled away in clouds of smoke, and now we saw, it was the head of Leviathan, his forehead was divided into streaks of green & purple like those on a tygers forehead: soon we saw his mouth & red gills hang just above the raging foam tinging the black deep with beams of blood, advancing toward us with all the fury of a spiritual existence.

My friend the Angel climb'd up from his station into the mill; I remain'd alone, & then this appearance was no more, but I found myself sitting on a pleasant bank beside a river by moon light hearing a harper who sung to the harp. & his theme was, The man who never alters his opinion is like standing water, & breeds reptiles of the mind.

But I arose, and sought for the mill & there I found my Angel, who surprised asked me, how I escaped?

I answerd. All that we saw was owing to your metaphysics; for when you ran away, I found myself on a bank by moonlight hearing a harper[28]

The implication is that Hell is a state of mind unique to each individual, echoing the famous lines from *Paradise Lost*: "The mind is its own place, and in it self/Can make a Heav'n of Hell, a Hell of Heav'n." Elsewhere, Blake claims Milton's success with *Paradise Lost* was due to infernal influence:

---

[28] Ibid.

34

*Note. The reason Milton wrote in fetters when he wrote of Angels
& God, and at liberty when of Devils & Hell, is because he was a
true Poet and of the Devil's party without knowing it*[29]

Unfortunately, *The Marriage of Heaven and Hell* initially received
very little exposure; the engraving and painting process was time-
consuming, and Blake only made nine copies of this manuscript.[30]

Percy Bysshe Shelley

English poet Percy Bysshe Shelley (1792-1822) played a central role in
establishing the genre of Romantic Satanism. He was the most prolific
author of the genre, and he also connected and interacted with the
other authors involved in the first wave of Romantic Satanism, having
met with Godwin, Southey, Blake, and Byron. He married Godwin's
daughter, Mary, in 1816, who made her own mark on the literary world
as the author of the horror novel *Frankenstein* (1818).

Shelley was also linked to the Johnson Circle by his reverence for
Milton's *Paradise Lost*. Shelley regarded Milton as the third great epic
poet, after Homer and Dante. In *A Defence of Poetry* (1821), Shelley
declares that Milton's Devil is morally superior to God:

> *Nothing can exceed the energy and magnificence of the character of
> Satan as expressed in* Paradise Lost. *It is a mistake to suppose that
> he could ever have been intended for the popular personification of
> evil. Implacable hate, patient cunning, and a sleepless refinement
> of device to inflict the extremist anguish on an enemy, these things*

---

[29] Ibid.

[30] William Blake, *William Blake: The Complete Illuminated Books* (New York, Thames &
Hudson, 2000), 106.

are evil; and, although venial in a slave, are not to be forgiven in a tyrant; although redeemed by much that ennobles his defeat in one subdued, are marked by all that dishonors his conquest in the victor. Milton's Devil as a moral being is as far superior to his God, as one who perseveres in some purpose which he has conceived to be excellent in spite of adversity and torture, is to one who in the cold security of undoubted triumph inflicts the most horrible revenge upon his enemy, not from any mistaken notion of inducing him to repent of a perseverance in enmity, but with the alleged design of exasperating him to deserve new torments. Milton has so far violated the popular creed (if this shall be judged to be a violation) as to have alleged no superiority of moral virtue to his God over his Devil. And this bold neglect of a direct moral purpose is the most decisive proof of the supremacy of Milton's genius. He mingled as it were the elements of human nature as colors upon a single pallet, and arranged them in the composition of his great picture according to the laws of epic truth; that is, according to the laws of that principle by which a series of actions of the external universe and of intelligent and ethical beings is calculated to excite the sympathy of succeeding generations of mankind.[31]

Here Shelley appreciates Milton's **normalization** of the Devil, his humanization of Satan by incorporating within him "the elements of human nature" in a manner "calculated to excite the sympathy of succeeding generations of mankind."[32] Shelley echoes this sentiment in *On the Devil, and Devils* (ca.1819):

---

[31] Percy Bysshe Shelley, "A Defense of Poetry," 2009, https://www.poetryfoundation.org/articles/69388/a-defence-of-poetry.

[32] In other words, Milton had sympathy for the Devil.

The Devil owes everything to Milton. ... Milton divested him of a sting, hoof, and horns, and clothed him with the sublime grandeur of a graceful but tremendous spirit.[33]

Unlike Blake and Byron, Shelley's contempt for Christianity developed at an early age and he held anti-Christian attitudes throughout his life. In 1811, Shelley was expelled from Oxford for writing "The Necessity of Atheism." The 19-year-old author brashly sent copies of the essay to all the college heads at Oxford, an essay which advocated not only atheism but also held that belief was an involuntary action:

Hence it is evident that, having no proofs from either of the three sources of conviction, the mind cannot believe the existence of a creative God: it is also evident that, as belief is a passion of the mind, no degree of criminality is attachable to disbelief; and that they only are reprehensible who neglect to remove the false medium through which their mind views any subject of discussion. Every reflecting mind must acknowledge that there is no proof of the existence of a Deity.[34]

In a note to *Queen Mab*, Shelley offers a dim view of Christianity:

The same means that have supported every other popular belief, have supported Christianity. War, imprisonment, assassination,

---

[33] Percy Bysshe Shelley, "On the Devil and Devils," in Harry Buxton Forman, Ed., *The Prose Works of Percy Bysshe Shelley* (London: Reeves and Turner, 1880), 390, https://en.wikisource.org/wiki/The_Prose_Works_of_Percy_Bysshe_Shelley/On_the_Devil,_and_Devils.

[34] Percy Bysshe Shelley, *Queen Mab* (London, W. Clark, 1821), 127-128, https://en.wikisource.org/wiki/Queen_Mab/Notes. Shelley republished the essay "The Necessity of Atheism" as a note to *Queen Mab* in 1813.

and falsehood; deeds of unexampled and incomparable atrocity have made it what it is. The blood shed by the votaries of the God of mercy and peace, since the establishment of his religion, would probably suffice to drown all other sectaries now on the habitable globe. We derive from our ancestors a faith thus fostered and supported: we quarrel, persecute, and hate for its maintenance.[35]

Shelley posited that Christianity was in decline:

Analogy seems to favour the opinion, that as, like other systems, Christianity has arisen and augmented, so like them it will decay and perish; that, as violence, darkness, and deceit, not reasoning and persuasion, have procured its admission among mankind, so, when enthusiasm has subsided, and time, that infallible, controverter of false opinions, has involved its pretended evidences in the darkness of antiquity, it will become obsolete; that Milton's poem alone will give permanency to the remembrance of its absurdities; and that men will laugh as heartily at grace, faith, redemption, and original sin, as they now do at the metamorphoses of Jupiter, the miracles of Romish saints, the efficacy of witchcraft, and the appearance of departed spirits.[36]

Finally, in his essay *On the Devil, and Devils* (c.1819), Shelley offered his own deconstruction of the Biblical myth of Satan that is reminiscent of the works of Paine and Voltaire discussed in the previous chapter:

To determine the nature and functions of the Devil, is no contemptible province of the European Mythology. Who, or what

---

[35] Shelley, *Queen Mab*, Note to Canto VII, 148-149.

[36] Ibid, 149-150.

he is, his origin, his habitation, his destiny, and his power, are
subjects which puzzle the most acute theologians, and on which no
orthodox person can be induced to give a decisive opinion. He is
the weak place of the popular religion—the vulnerable belly of the
crocodile.[37]

The implication is that if one can deconstruct the myth of the Devil and explain it away, the whole edifice of Christian theology will collapse. Shelley's essay thus examines the origin and nature of the Devil, and attempts to determine the locations of Heaven and Hell with the purpose of discrediting Christianity.

Shelley authored a number of works of Romantic Satanism. We will examine four of his most significant works in the genre: *The Devil's Walk, Queen Mab, The Revolt of Islam,* and *Prometheus Unbound*

The Devil's Walk

Shelley's first work in the genre of Romantic Satanism was the poem *The Devil's Walk* (1812). Schock puts this work into perspective:

Shelley modeled this poem on the collaborative ballad by Southey
and Coleridge, 'The Devil's Thoughts,' which he must have
seen when he visited Southey at Keswick in late 1811. The
narrative donne of Southey's ballad—the Devil's tour of his earthly
kingdom—offered the vehicle for satiric imitation.[38]

The Devil's Walk **normalizes** the Devil, disguising him so he can walk among the people of London unnoticed... and attend church!

---

[37] Shelley, "On the Devil, and Devils," 383.

[38] Schock, *Romanitc Satanism,* 81-82.

Once, early in the morning, Beelzebub arose,
  With care his sweet person adorning,
  He put on his Sunday clothes.

He drew on a boot to hide his hoof,
  He drew on a glove to hide his claw,
  His horns were concealed by a Bras Chapeau,
  And the Devil went forth as natty a Beau
  As Bond-street ever saw.

He sate him down, in London town,
  Before earth's morning ray;
  With a favourite imp he began to chat,
  On religion, and scandal, this and that,
  Until the dawn of day.

And then to St. James's Court he went,
  And St. Paul's Church he took on his way;
  He was mighty thick with every Saint,
  Though they were formal and he was gay.
  . . . .
A Priest, at whose elbow the Devil during prayer
Sate familiarly, side by side,
Declared that, if the Tempter were there,
His presence he would not abide.
Ah! ah! thought Old Nick, that's a very stale trick,
For without the Devil, O favourite of Evil,
In your carriage you would not ride.[39]

---

[39] Percy Bysshe Shelley, *The Devil's* Walk, 2013, https://en.wikisource.org/wiki/The_Devil%27s_Walk_(Shelley).

Shelley's satire casts the Devil as a farmer who watches over his cattle, the poor and the oppressed members of the human race. His herds are managed by the oppressors of the people, particularly by members of the British Government that are mocked in the poem. Satan calls George III a brainless king and the Prince Regent a fat, spoiled little boy, and implies that the King, Regent, and other members of the government were easily manipulated to do his bidding:

> *Ah! ah! thought Satan, the pasture is good,*
>   *My Cattle will here thrive better than others;*
>   *They dine on news of human blood,*
>   *They sup on the groans of the dying and dead,*
>   *And supperless never will go to bed;*
>   *Which will make them fat as their brothers.*
>   *. . . . .*
>   *For they thrive well whose garb of gore*
>   *Is Satan's choicest livery,*
>   *And they thrive well who from the poor*
>   *Have snatched the bread of penury,*
>   *And heap the houseless wanderer's store*
>   *On the rank pile of luxury.*
>
> *The Bishops thrive, though they are big;*
>   *The Lawyers thrive, though they are thin;*
>   *For every gown, and every wig,*
>   *Hides the safe thrift of Hell within.*[40]

Satan is so elated with all the pain and misery they cause that he casts off his disguise:

---

[40] Shelley, *The Devil's Walk.*

Oh! why is the Father of Hell in such glee,
  As he grins from ear to ear?
  Why does he doff his clothes joyfully,
  As he skips, and prances, and flaps his wing,
  As he sidles, leers, and twirls his sting,
  And dares, as he is, to appear?

A statesman passed—alone to him,
  The Devil dare his whole shape uncover,
  To show each feature, every limb,
  Secure of an unchanging lover.

At this known sign, a welcome sight,
  The watchful demons sought their King,
  And every Fiend of the Stygian night,
  Was in an instant on the wing.

Pale Loyalty, his guilt-steeled brow,
  With wreaths of gory laurel crowned:
  The hell-hounds, Murder, Want and Woe,
  Forever hungering, flocked around;
  From Spain had Satan sought their food,
  'Twas human woe and human blood![41]

At the end of the poem, Shelley brings Satan's empire down:

Hark! the earthquake's crash I hear,—
  Kings turn pale, and Conquerors start,
  Ruffians tremble in their fear,

---

[41] Ibid.

For their Satan doth depart.

This day Fiends give to revelry
To celebrate their King's return,
And with delight its Sire to see
Hell's adamantine limits burn.

But were the Devil's sight as keen
As Reason's penetrating eye,
His sulphurous Majesty I ween,
Would find but little cause for joy.

For the sons of Reason see
That, ere fate consume the Pole,
The false Tyrant's cheek shall be
Bloodless as his coward soul.[42]

The power of Reason will destroy Satan and the oppressors of mankind, suggestive of the Enlightenment-inspired American and French Revolutions. Shelley's identification of Satan with the oppressors of the people is unusual; in most of his subsequent works within the genre of Romantic Satanism, the Satanic figure is oppressed and rebels against an unjust God.

Queen Mab

Queen Mab, a Philosophical Poem (1813) was Shelley's first major poem. Queen Mab takes the spirit of Lanthe (the name of Shelley's eldest child) on a journey through time and space, recounting the evils of

---

[42] Ibid.

monarchy, commerce, and religion found in the past and present, and presenting a utopian vision of a society free from those institutions before returning her to her body. It also included a large section of notes that deconstructed Christianity and advocated free love, atheism, and vegetarianism.

In the seventh canto, the fairy queen summons up the phantom of Ahasuerus, the Wandering Jew of Christian legend recounted in a note by Shelley:

> *Near two thousand years have elapsed since he was first goaded by never-ending restlessness, to rove the globe from pole to pole. When our Lord was wearied with the burthen of his ponderous cross, and wanted to rest before the door of Ahasuerus, the unfeeling wretch drove him away with brutality. The Saviour of mankind staggered, sinking under the heavy load, but uttered no complaint. An angel of death appeared before Ahasuerus, and exclaimed indignantly, "Barbarian! thou hast denied rest to the Son of Man: be it denied thee also, until he comes to judge the world."*
>
> *A black demon, let loose from hell upon Ahasuerus, goads him now from country to country; he is denied the consolation which death affords, and precluded from the rest of the peaceful grave.*[43]

The monologue of Ahasuerus delivers a scathing attack on Christianity, using the themes of **Inversion** and **Reinterpretation** to present the Bible in negative terms:

> *Spirit: Is there a God?*
> *Ahasuerus: Is there a God?—aye, an almighty God,*
> *And vengeful as almighty! Once his voice*

---

[43] Shelley, *Queen Mab*, Note VII, 143.

Was heard on earth: earth shuddered at the sound;
The fiery-visaged firmament expressed
Abhorrence, and the grave of nature yawned
To swallow all the dauntless and the good
That dared to hurl defiance at his throne,
Girt as it was with power. None but slaves
Survived,—cold-blooded slaves, who did the work
Of tyrannous omnipotence; whose souls
No honest indignation ever urged
To elevated daring, to one deed
Which gross and sensual self did not pollute.
These slaves built temples for the omnipotent,
Gorgeous and vast: the costly altars smoked
With human blood, and hideous pæans rung
Through all the long-drawn aisles.
These were Jehovah's words.
From an eternity of idleness
I, God, awoke; in seven days' toil made earth
From nothing; rested, and created man:
I placed him in a paradise, and there
Planted the tree of evil, so that he
Might eat and perish, and my soul procure
Wherewith to sate its malice, and to turn,
Even like a heartless conqueror of the earth,
All misery to my fame. The race of men
Chosen to my honour, with impunity
May sate the lusts I planted in their heart.
Here I command thee hence to lead them on,
Until, with hardened feet, their conquering troops
Wade on the promised soil through woman's blood,
And make my name be dreaded through the land.

Yet ever burning flame and ceaseless woe
Shall be the doom of their eternal souls,
With every soul on this ungrateful earth,
Virtuous or vicious, weak or strong,—even all
Shall perish, to fulfil the blind revenge
(Which you, to men, call justice) of their God.

Ahasuerus continues his tirade, characterizing the enslaved worshipers of God as violent murderers:

Yes! I have seen God's worshippers unsheathe
The sword of his revenge, when grace descended,
Confirming all unnatural impulses,
To sanctify their desolating deeds;
And frantic priests waved the ill-omened cross
O'er the unhappy earth: then shone the Sun
On showers of gore from the upflashing steel
Of safe assassination, and all crime
Made stingless by the spirits of the Lord,
And blood-red rainbows canopied the land.
Spirit! no year of my eventful being
Has passed unstained by crime and misery,
Which flows from God's own faith.[44]

The theme of **Revolution** comes into play when Ahasuerus expresses his desire to rebel against God, reminiscent of Milton's Satan:

But my soul,
From sight and sense of the polluting woe

---

[44] Shelley, *Queen Mab*, Canto VII, 64-69.

46

Of tyranny, had long learned to prefer
Hell's freedom to the servitude of heaven.
Therefore I rose, and dauntlessly began
My lonely and unending pilgrimage,
Resolved to wage unweariable war
With my almighty tyrant, and to hurl
Defiance at his impotence to harm
Beyond the curse I bore. The very hand
That barred my passage to the peaceful grave
Has crushed the earth to misery, and given
Its empire to the chosen of his slaves.
These have I seen, even from the earliest dawn
Of weak, unstable, and precarious power;
Then preaching peace, as now they practise war,
So, when they turned but from the massacre
Of unoffending infidels, to quench
Their thirst for ruin in the very blood
That flowed in their own veins, and pityless zeal
Froze every human feeling[45]

Note the allusion to Satan's famous statement from *Paradise Lost*: "Better to reign in Hell than serve in Heaven." Shelley made many allusions to Milton's poem in *Queen Mab*.

Ahasuerus' desire to rebel is also stated at the conclusion of his monologue:

Thus have I stood,—through a wild waste of years
Struggling with whirlwinds of mad agony,
Yet peaceful, and serene, and self-enshrined,

---

[45] Ibid, 68.

Mocking my powerless tyrant's horrible curse
With stubborn and unalterable will,
Even as a giant oak, which heaven's fierce flame
Had scathed in the wilderness, to stand
A monument of fadeless ruin there;
Yet peacefully and movelessly it braves
The midnight conflict of the wintry storm,
As in the sun-light's calm it spreads
Its worn and withered arms on high
To meet the quiet of a summer's noon.[46]

Shelley's Satanic Ahasuerus defies and mocks the malevolent God that has cursed him to wander the Earth. His body must eternally roam, but the mind and spirit of Ahasuerus are immovable like a giant oak, which stands firm amidst God's "polluting woe of tyranny" that has "crushed the earth to misery." Shelley reveals that in denying him eternal rest, God has made Ahasuerus the eternal witness to his divine crimes.

The Revolt of Islam

The Revolt of Islam (1818), Shelley's longest poem, was originally published under the title *Laon and Cythna; or The Revolution of the Golden City: A Vision of the Nineteenth Century*. The title was changed after the publisher asked Shelley to change some of the more provocative parts of the story, particularly the incestuous relationship between the two main characters. The poem has little to do with Islam; Shelley likely chose a Muslim country instead of a Christian one to avoid censorship for the anti-religious tone of the work.

In the first canto, the narrator of the poem witnesses an arduous

---

[46] Ibid, 70.

battle between an eagle and a snake. After a long struggle the snake
falls in the ocean; a woman on the shore takes the wounded snake in
her embrace. She invites the narrator to join her on a voyage, and then
explains the significance of the battle they just witnessed by describing
the nature of the universe:

> *Speak not to me, but hear! Much shalt thou learn,*
> *Much must remain unthought, and more untold,*
> *In the dark Future's ever-flowing urn:*
> *Know then, that from the depth of ages old*
> *Two Powers o'er mortal things dominion hold,*
> *Ruling the world with a divided lot,*
> *Immortal, all-pervading, manifold,*
> *Twin Genii, equal Gods—when life and thought*
> *Sprang forth, they burst the womb of inessential Naught.*
>
> *The earliest dweller of the world alone,*
> *Stood on the verge of chaos: Lo! afar*
> *O'er the wide wild abyss two meteors shone,*
> *Sprung from the depth of its tempestuous jar:*
> *A blood-red Comet and the Morning Star*
> *Mingling their beams in combat—as he stood,*
> *All thoughts within his mind waged mutual war,*
> *In dreadful sympathy—when to the flood*
> *That fair Star fell, he turn'd and shed his brother's blood*
>
> *Thus evil triumph'd, and the Spirit of evil,*
> *One Power of many shapes which none may know,*
> *One Shape of many names; the Fiend did revel*
> *In victory, reigning o'er a world of woe,*
> *For the new race of man went to and fro,*

Famish'd and homeless, loathed and loathing, wild,
And hating good—for his immortal foe,
He changed from starry shape, beauteous and mild,
To a dire Snake, with man and beast unreconciled.

The darkness lingering o'er the dawn of things,
    Was Evil's breath and life: this made him strong
    To soar aloft with overshadowing wings;
    And the great Spirit of Good did creep among
    The nations of mankind, and every tongue
    Cursed and blasphemed him as he passed; for none
    Knew good from evil, though their names were hung
    In mockery o'er the fane where many a groan,
    As King, and Lord, and God, the conquering Fiend did own.

The Fiend, whose name was Legion: Death, Decay,
    Earthquake and Blight, and Want, and Madness pale,
    Winged and wan diseases, an array
    Numerous as leaves that strew the autumnal gale;
    Poison, a snake in flowers, beneath the veil
    Of food and mirth, hiding his mortal head;
    And, without whom all these might naught avail,
    Fear, Hatred, Faith, and Tyranny, who spread
    Those subtle nets which snare the living and the dead.[47]

Here, Shelley describes an **inversion** of good and evil forces inspired by Gnostic dualism. The poem connects the serpent with the Morning Star, Lucifer, and the Spirit of Good; the eagle, God, is the Spirit of Evil,

---

[47] Percy Bysshe Shelley, *The Revolt of Islam*, Canto I, Stanzas xxv-xxix, 2019, https://en.wikisource.org/wiki/The_Revolt_of_Islam/Canto_I.

the Fiend who tortures humanity. The theme of **revolution** is also present, both in the struggle between the serpent and the eagle—"The Snake and Eagle meet—the world's foundations tremble!"—and the main conflict of the poem.

The boat docks at the Temple of the Spirit of Good "such as mortal hand has never built" and the narrator is led to a vast hall with a thousand columns and an empty throne. The woman and serpent walk in, then mystically combine into a radiant and majestic form (suggesting Lucifer) that says:

> *Thou must a listener be*
> *This day—two mighty Spirits now return,*
> *Like birds of calm, from the world's raging sea,*
> *They pour fresh light from Hope's immortal urn;*
> *A tale of human power—despair not—list and learn!*[48]

The main part of the poem tells the story of two lovers, Laon and Cythna, and their aspirations to rid the fictional country Argolis from the tyrant Othman with a bloodless revolution. The connection between our protagonists and Lucifer is only implied yet obvious.

Laon and Cythna succeed in driving the tyrant out of the Golden City without warfare, but the next day foreign armies arrive to assist Othman and slaughter the revolutionaries. Plague and famine follow, and it is decided that Laon and Cythna must be sacrificed to appease the gods. Laon turns himself in on the condition that Cythna is given free passage out of the country, but as Laon is being burned at the stake, Cythna rides up to join him, and they die together. They wake up in paradise, where a boat appears to take them to the Temple of the Spirit of Good; as they approach the Temple, the poem ends.

---

[48] Shelley, *The Revolt of Islam*, Canto I, Stanza lvii.

Per Faxneld heralds *The Revolt of Islam* as a work of Satanic Feminism, where "Shelley's revolutionary Satanism is combined with what can, without much hesitation, be described as a feminist ideal."[49] Cythna fights not just for liberty but for the liberation of women: "Can man be free if woman be a slave?" In the sixth canto, Cythna rescues Laon from members of the foreign army, a complete and surprising reversal of traditional 19th century gender roles:

> *...of those brave bands*
> *I soon survived alone—and now I lay*
> *Vanquished and faint, the grasp of bloody hands*
> *I felt, and saw on high the glare of falling brands,*
> *When on my foes a sudden terror came,*
> *And they fled, scattering.—Lo! with reinless speed*
> *A black Tartarian horse of giant frame,*
> *Comes trampling over the dead; the living bleed*
> *Beneath the hoofs of that tremendous steed,*
> *On which, like to an Angel, robed in white,*
> *Sate one waving a sword; the hosts recede*
> *And fly, as through their ranks, with awful might*
> *Sweeps in the shadow of eve that Phantom swift and bright;*[50]

Her account of the rescue is decisive and heroic:

> *Friend, thy bands were losing*
> *The battle, as I stood before the King*
> *In bonds. I burst them then, and, swiftly choosing*

---

[49] Per Faxneld, *Satanic Feminism: Lucifer as the Liberator of Woman in Nineteenth-Century Culture* (New York, Oxford University Press, 2017), 84.

[50] Shelley, *The Revolt of Islam*, Canto VI, Stanzas xx-xix.

The time, did seize a Tartar's sword, and spring
Upon his horse, and swift as on the whirlwind's wing
Have thou and I been borne beyond pursuer,
And we are here.[51]

Faxneld concludes:

> *Percy Bysshe Shelley, the prime mover in the creation of literary*
> *Satanism, was a feminist. In* The Revolt of Islam *(1818) he merges*
> *the two. The Satanically inspired female revolutionary in this*
> *narrative declares that the emancipation of women is a prerequisite*
> *for the true liberation of mankind. Hence,* The Revolt of Islam,
> *with its frank combining of equally unequivocal Satanism and*
> *feminism, makes Percy Shelley the first Satanic feminist.*[52]

Prometheus Unbound

Shelley's last work of Romantic Satanism was *Prometheus Unbound* (1820). The title alludes to a trilogy of plays attributed to Aeschylus, the father of Greek tragedy: *Prometheus Bound, Prometheus Unbound* and *Prometheus the Fire-Bearer*. Only the first play survived; the others exist only in fragments. *Prometheus Bound* tells the story of the imprisonment and torture of the titan Prometheus, while Shelley's *Prometheus Unbound* tells the story of his release. By expressing the theme of **inversion** in terms of a Greek play, Shelley sought to avoid censors.

In his preface to the play, Shelley compares his Prometheus with Milton's Satan:

---

[51] Ibid, Stanzas xxv-xxvi.

[52] Faxneld, *Satanic Feminism*, 496.

The only imaginary being resembling in any degree Prometheus is Satan; and Prometheus is, in my judgement, a more poetical character than Satan, because, in addition to courage, and majesty, and firm and patient opposition to omnipotent force, he is susceptible of being described as exempt from the taints of ambition, envy, revenge, and a desire for personal aggrandizement, which, in the hero of Paradise Lost, interfere with the interest. The character of Satan engenders in the mind a pernicious casuistry which leads us to weigh his faults with his wrongs, and to excuse the former because the latter exceed all measure. In the minds of those who consider that magnificent fiction with a religious feeling it engenders something worse. But Prometheus is, as it were, the type of the highest perfection of moral and intellectual nature, impelled by the purest and the truest motives to the best and noblest ends.[53]

Shelley uses the themes of **inversion** and **revolution** to frame the conflict between Prometheus and Jupiter. In the poem, the Satanic titan Prometheus has been punished for his opposition to the tyrannical god Jupiter. Jupiter is cast as the oppressor of humanity and the source of all the problems in the world; Prometheus is the savior of humanity, who gave them fire and knowledge and was punished for his transgression.

PROMETHEUS:
  Monarch of Gods and Dæmons,[54] *and all Spirits*
  But One, who throng those bright and rolling worlds
  Which Thou and I alone of living things
  Behold with sleepless eyes! regard this Earth

---

[53] Percy Bysshe Shelley, *Prometheus Unbound*, Preface, (London, C and J Ollier, 1820), http://knarf.english.upenn.edu/PShelley/promtp.html

[54] Daemons: spiritual intermediaries between gods and men.

Made multitudinous with thy slaves, whom thou
Requitest for knee-worship, prayer, and praise,
And toil, and hecatombs[55] of broken hearts,
With fear and self-contempt and barren hope;
Whilst me, who am thy foe, eyeless in hate,
Hast thou made reign and triumph, to thy scorn,
O'er mine own misery and thy vain revenge.
Three thousand years of sleep-unsheltered hours,
And moments aye[56] divided by keen pangs
Till they seemed years, torture and solitude,
Scorn and despair—these are mine empire:
More glorious far than that which thou surveyest
From thine unenvied throne, O Mighty God!
Almighty, had I deigned to share the shame
Of thine ill tyranny, and hung not here
Nailed to this wall of eagle-baffling mountain,
Black, wintry, dead, unmeasured; without herb,
Insect, or beast, or shape or sound of life.
Ah me! alas, pain, pain ever, forever![57]

In Act II, the actions that led to Prometheus' imprisonment are recounted:

Then Prometheus
  Gave wisdom, which is strength, to Jupiter,
  And with this law alone, 'Let man be free,'
  Clothed him with the dominion of wide Heaven.

---

[55] Hecatombs: sacrifices of many victims made as an offering.

[56] Aye: continually.

[57] Shelley, *Prometheus Unbound*, Act I, lines 1-23.

To know nor faith, nor love, nor law, to be
Omnipotent but friendless, is to reign;
And Jove now reigned; for on the race of man
First famine, and then toil, and then disease,
Strife, wounds, and ghastly death unseen before,
Fell; and the unseasonable seasons drove,
With alternating shafts of frost and fire,
Their shelterless, pale tribes to mountain caves;
And in their desert hearts fierce wants he sent,
And mad disquietudes, and shadows idle
Of unreal good, which levied mutual war,
So ruining the lair wherein they raged.[58]

Witnessing Jupiter's abuse of power, Prometheus seeks to alleviate humanity's suffering by offering them the gift of wisdom, the crime against Jupiter that leads to his imprisonment:

And he tamed fire which, like some beast of prey,
Most terrible, but lovely, played beneath
The frown of man; and tortured to his will
Iron and gold, the slaves and signs of power,
And gems and poisons, and all subtlest forms
Hidden beneath the mountains and the waves.
He gave man speech, and speech created thought,
Which is the measure of the universe;
And Science struck the thrones of earth and heaven,
Which shook, but fell not; and the harmonious mind
Poured itself forth in all-prophetic song;
And music lifted up the listening spirit

---

[58] Shelley, *Prometheus Unbound*, Act II, lines 43-58.

Until it walked, exempt from mortal care,
Godlike, o'er the clear billows of sweet sound;
And human hands first mimicked and then mocked,
With moulded limbs more lovely than its own,
The human form, till marble grew divine;
And mothers, gazing, drank the love men see
Reflected in their race, behold, and perish.
He told the hidden power of herbs and springs,
And Disease drank and slept. Death grew like sleep.
He taught the implicated orbits woven
Of the wide-wandering stars; and how the sun
Changes his lair, and by what secret spell
The pale moon is transformed, when her broad eye
Gazes not on the interlunar sea.
He taught to rule, as life directs the limbs,
The tempest-winged chariots of the Ocean,
And the Celt knew the Indian. Cities then
Were built, and through their snow-like columns flowed
The warm winds, and the azure ether shone,
And the blue sea and shadowy hills were seen.
Such, the alleviations of his state,
Prometheus gave to man, for which he hangs
Withering in destined pain[59]

Prometheus may have originally been a Satanic rebel, but Prometheus has nothing to do with the fall of Jupiter in the play. Jupiter is brought down by Demogorgon, his offspring with Themis, as prophesied in Greek myth. Prometheus is freed by Hercules after the fact. There is no battle, no reconciliation between Prometheus and Jupiter. The titan's

---

[59] Ibid, lines 66-100.

past and attitude are Satanic, but his inaction is not.

When Jupiter is overthrown, humanity, no longer under his evil influence, becomes free:

> *The painted veil, by those who were, called life,*
> *Which mimicked, as with colours idly spread,*
> *All men believed or hoped, is torn aside;*
> *The loathsome mask has fallen, the man remains*
> *Sceptreless, free, uncircumscribed, but man*
> *Equal, unclassed, tribeless, and nationless,*
> *Exempt from awe, worship, degree, the king*
> *Over himself; just, gentle, wise: but man*
> *Passionless? — no, yet free from guilt or pain*[60]

At the end of the play, Demogorgon offers advice in the spirit of Romantic Satanism:

> *To suffer woes which Hope thinks infinite;*
> *To forgive wrongs darker than death or night;*
> *To defy Power, which seems omnipotent;*
> *To love, and bear; to hope till Hope creates*
> *From its own wreck the thing it contemplates;*
> *Neither to change, nor falter, nor repent;*
> *This, like thy glory, Titan, is to be*
> *Good, great and joyous, beautiful and free;*
> *This is alone Life; Joy, Empire, and Victory!*[61]

Shelley's numerous works featuring Satan and Satanic themes played a

---

[60] Shelley, *Prometheus Unbound*, Act III, lines 190-204.

[61] Shelley, *Prometheus Unbound*, Act IV, lines 570-578.

significant role in establishing and developing the genre of Romantic Satanism. He died a month short of his 30th birthday, drowning in a tragic boating accident off the coast of Italy that cut short the promising career of one of England's most celebrated poets. One can only wonder how many more works of Romantic Satanism Shelley would have created had he survived.

Lord Byron

George Gordon, Lord Byron (1788-1824) was the most well-known of the English Romantic Satanists during the Regency, noted for both his poetry and his many love affairs. His early works, such as *Childe Harold's Pilgrimage* (1812), *The Giaour* (1813), and *The Siege of Corinth* (1815) made him a celebrity; his neglect of his wife and daughter during his many public affairs, including an incestuous relationship with his half-sister, made him an outcast in English society. These scandals and significant debts forced him to leave England in 1816, never to return. Byron spent the rest of his life traveling and living in various places within Continental Europe while writing poetry that would maintain his fame in literary and social circles. He died in 1824 of fever contracted while fighting for Greek independence from the Ottoman Empire.

Byron wrote a few works with Satanic themes; here we will examine two of his most significant works in the genre of Romantic Satanism, *Manfred* and *Cain*.

Manfred

Byron's first dramatic work was *Manfred* (1817). As a dramatic poem, it was meant to be read, not staged. It tells the story of a guilt-ridden Manfred, who seeks death to end his sorrow. The theme of this work is

revolution, as Manfred rebels against agents of God, Satan, and other supernatural forces, refusing to serve them or yield to them in death, finally dying on his own terms.

The work is divided into three acts; the setting is high in the Alps, where Manfred has a castle. In the first act, Manfred, deep in despair, calls on the spirits to help him forget; what he wishes to forget is not named. They reveal that death can make him forget, but as immortal spirits, they cannot help him die. Manfred prepares to jump off a cliff when he is saved by a hunter.

In Act II, the hunter tries to help Manfred, but Manfred, tortured with guilt, still seeks death. He leaves the hunter and summons the Witch of the Alps for aid. Manfred reveals that he fell in love with a woman, Astarte; it is implied that he had an incestuous affair with his sister, and their affair led to her death. When Manfred asks the witch to either resurrect his sister or reunite them in death, she agrees to help, but only if he swears obedience to her. Manfred is defiant:

> *I will not swear – Obey! and whom? the spirits*
> *Whose presence I command, and be the slave*
> *Of those who served me – Never!*[62]

The Witch disappears.

In the last scene of Act II, Manfred enters the "Hall of Arimanes" facing "Arimanes on his Throne, a Globe of Fire, surrounded by the Spirits," who praise him as the master of death and destruction:

> *Hymn of the Spirits.*

---

[62] Lord Byron, *Manfred*, Act 2, Scene 2, lines 169-171, in Charles W. Eliot, Ed., *The Harvard Classics*, Vol. XVIII, Part 6 (New York, P.F. Collier & Son, 1914), https://www.bartleby.com/br/01806.html.

Hail to our Master–Prince of Earth and Air!
Who walks the clouds and waters–in his hand
The sceptre of the elements, which tear
Themselves to chaos at his high command!
He breatheth–and a tempest shakes the sea;
He speaketh–and the clouds reply in thunder;
He gazeth – from his glance the sunbeams flee;
He moveth – earthquakes rend the world asunder.
Beneath his footsteps the volcanoes rise;
His shadow is the Pestilence; his path
The comets herald through the burning skies,
And planets turn to ashes at his wrath.
To him War offers daily sacrifice;
To him Death pays his tribute; Life is his,
With all its infinite of agonies –
And his the spirit of whatever is![63]

Don't be surprised if this sounds like Satan in Hell. The name Arimanes is derived from Ahriman, the personification of evil in Zoroastrianism, a religion that predates Christianity. Ahriman shares many attributes with the Christian Satan, and the former may have been an influence on the latter.

Manfred refuses to bow down before the fearsome Arimanes, even when threatened by the spirits. Manfred asks Arimanes to summon the spirit of Astarte so Manfred can converse with her. When Astarte appears, Manfred begs her to speak with him, to forgive him or condemn him. Astarte hails Manfred and tells him that he will die tomorrow, then disappears. Manfred departs.

Act III takes place in Manfred's castle, where Manfred waits for the

---

[63] Byron, *Manfred*, Act 2, Scene 4, lines 1-17.

setting sun and prepares for his immanent death. He receives a visit from the Abbot of St. Maurice, who is troubled by rumors that Manfred was conversing with evil spirits. The Abbot tries to save Manfred's soul, but Manfred refuses:

Abbot: I come to save, and not destroy –
I would not pry into thy secret soul;
But if these things be sooth, there still is time
For penitence and pity; reconcile thee
With the true church, and through the church to heaven.

Manfred: I hear thee. This is my reply. Whate'er
I may have been or am doth rest between
Heaven and myself. – I shall not choose a mortal
To be my mediator. Have I sinned
Against your ordinances? Prove and punish!

Abbot: My son! I did not speak of punishment,
But patience and pardon;–with thyself
The choice of such remains – and for the last,
Our institutions and our strong belief
Have given me power to smooth the path from sin
To higher hope and better thoughts; the first
I leave to heaven – "Vengeance is mine alone"
So saith the Lord, and with all humbleness
His servant echoes back the awful word.

Manfred: Old Man! there is no power in holy men,
Nor charm in prayer – nor purifying form,
Nor penitence – nor outward look – nor fast –
Nor agony – nor, greater than all these,

The inward tortures of that deep despair,
Which is remorse, without the fear of hell,
But all in all sufficient to itself
Would make a hell of heaven–can exorcise
From out the unbounded spirit the quick sense
Of its own sins, wrongs, sufferance, and revenge
Upon itself; there is no future pang
Can deal that justice on the self–condemned
He deals on his own soul.[64]

In the final scene, the Abbot returns to try and save Manfred one more time, but a spirit of Hell appears and threatens to drag Manfred away:

Spirit: Come!

Abbot: What art thou, unknown being? Answer! Speak!

Spirit: The genius of this mortal. Come! 'tis time.

Manfred: I am prepared for all things, but deny
The power which summons me. Who sent thee here?

Spirit: Thou'lt know anon – Come! Come!

Manfred: I have commanded
Things of an essence greater far than thine,
And striven with thy masters. Get thee hence!

Spirit: Mortal! thine hour has come. Away, I say.

---

[64] Byron, *Manfred*, Act 3, Scene 1, lines 60-91.

Manfred: I knew and know my hour is come, but not
   To render up my soul to such as thee:
   Away! I'll die as I have lived – alone.

Spirit: Then I must summon up my brethren.–Rise!

Other Spirits rise up.

Abbot: Avaunt! Ye evil ones! Avaunt! I say, –
   Ye have no power where piety hath power,
   And I do charge ye in the name–

Spirit: Old Man!
   We know ourselves, our mission, and thine order;
   Waste not thy pious words on idle uses,
   It were in vain; this man is forfeited.
   Once more, I summon him! Away! Away!

Manfred: I do defy ye, – though I feel my soul
   Is ebbing from me, yet I do defy ye;
   Nor will I hence while I have earthly breath
   To breathe my scorn upon ye – earthly strength
   To wrestle, though with spirits; what ye take
   Shall be ta'en limb by limb.

Spirit: Reluctant Mortal!
   Is this the Magian who would so pervade
   The world invisible, and make himself
   Almost our equal?–Can it be that thou
   Art thus in love with life? The very life
   Which made thee wretched!

Manfred: Thou false fiend! thou liest!
My life is in its last hour – that I know,
Nor would redeem a moment of that hour;
I do not combat against death, but thee
And thy surrounding angels; my past power
Was purchased by no compact with thy crew,
But by superior science – penance – daring –
And length of watching – strength of mind – and skill
In knowledge of our fathers – when the earth
Saw men and spirits walking side by side,
And gave ye no supremacy: I stand
Upon my strength – I do defy – deny –
Spurn back, and scorn ye! –

Spirit: But thy many crimes
Have made thee – – –

Manfred: What are they to such as thee?
Must crimes be punished but by other crimes,
And greater criminals? Back to thy hell!
Thou hast no power upon me, that I feel;
Thou never shalt possess me, that I know:
What I have done is done; I bear within
A torture which could nothing gain from thine:
The mind which is immortal makes itself
Requital for its good or evil thoughts –
Is its own origin of ill and end –

And its own place and time[65] – its innate sense,
When stripped of this mortality, derives
No colour from the fleeting things without,
But is absorbed in sufferance or in joy,
Born from the knowledge of its own desert.
Thou didst not tempt me, and thou couldst not tempt me;
I have not been thy dupe, nor am thy prey,
But was my own destroyer, and will be
My own hereafter. – Back, ye baffled fiends!
The hand of death is on me – but not yours![66]

The demons depart without Manfred's soul and Manfred dies, defiant to the very end.

The character of Manfred has its roots in the misfortunes of Byron's life. In 1816, after a failed marriage, Byron was caught having an incestuous affair with his half-sister Augusta. When the scandalous affair was revealed, Byron, ostracized by most of his friends and heavily in debt, left England for Switzerland and never returned. The affair and the grief it caused Byron are on display in Manfred.

Many scholars consider the character of Manfred to be the ultimate expression of the Byronic hero: a melancholy and arrogant antihero, attractive and intelligent, yet dark, rebellious, and moody. Byronic heroes are haunted by a terrible wrong or secret love from their past, and their rejection of social conventions and norms alienate them from others. They are often reckless, self-destructive, and self-centered, yet behave heroically. Manfred possesses all of these qualities.

---

[65] Compare with Milton, *Paradise Lost*, Book 1, lines 253-255: "A mind not to be chang'd by Place or Time./The mind is its own place, and in itself/Can make a Heaven of Hell, and a Hell of Heaven."

[66] Byron, *Manfred*, Act 3, Scene 4, lines 94-162.

Scholars have also noted the similarities between Manfred and Milton's Satan. Both are sympathetic rebels against overwhelming and oppressive forces, with Satan opposing God and Manfred opposing the supernatural entities of death. Byron makes allusions to *Paradise Lost*, especially in the final scene, that strengthen the bond between two characters.

Cain

Byron wrote and published *Cain, A Mystery*, in 1821. The work is a closet drama, meaning it is meant to be read rather than performed on a stage. *Cain* is written in the style and spirit of the mystery plays of the Middle Ages, plays based on stories from the Bible. Byron's *Cain* is a **reinterpretation** of the story of Cain and Abel from the perspective of its antagonist.

In his preface to the play, Byron states that the serpent of Genesis has nothing to do with Lucifer:

> *The reader will recollect that the book of Genesis does not state that Eve was tempted by a demon, but by "The Serpent" and that only because he was "the most subtil of all the beasts of the field."*
> *.... If [Lucifer] disclaims having tempted Eve in the shape of the Serpent, it is only because the book of Genesis has not the most distant allusion to anything of the kind, but merely to the Serpent in his Serpentine capacity.*[67]

In the first act, Adam and his family are offering a sacrifice to God, but Cain refuses to participate, angry that the actions of God and his parents

---

[67] Lord Byron, *Cain, A Mystery*, Preface. PDF, Peter Cochran, Ed, http://newsteadabbey-byronsociety.org/works/poems.htm.

have cursed him to toil and die outside Eden. Lucifer approaches, claiming Cain shall live forever. Cain is skeptical:

Cain: ...and thou, with all thy might, what art thou?

Lucifer: One who aspired to be what made thee, and
    Would not have made thee what thou art.

Cain: Ah!
    Thou look'st almost a god; and –

Lucifer: I am none:
    And having failed to be one, would be nought
    Save what I am. He conquered; let him reign!

Cain: Who?

Lucifer: Thy Sire's Maker – and the Earth's.

Cain: And Heaven's
    And all that in them is. So I have heard
    His Seraphs sing; and so my father saith.

Lucifer: They say – what they must sing and say, on pain
    Of being that which I am, – and thou art –
    Of Spirits and of men.

Cain: And what is that?

Lucifer: Souls who dare use their immortality –
    Souls who dare look the Omnipotent tyrant in

His everlasting face, and tell him that
His evil is not good! If he has made,
As he saith – which I know not, nor believe –
But, if he made us – he cannot unmake:
We are immortal! – nay, he'd have us so,
That he may torture – let him! He is great –
But, in his greatness, is no happier than
We in our conflict! Goodness would not make
Evil; and what else hath he made? But let him
Sit on his vast and solitary throne,
Creating worlds, to make Eternity
Less burthensome to his immense existence
And unparticipated solitude;
Let him crowd orb on orb: he is alone
Indefinite, Indissoluble Tyrant;
Could he but crush himself, 'twere the best boon
He ever granted: but let him reign on!
And multiply himself in misery!
Spirits and Men, at least we sympathise –
And, suffering in concert, make our pangs
Innumerable, more endurable,
By the unbounded sympathy of all
With all! But He! so wretched in his height,
So restless in his wretchedness, must still
Create, and re-create – perhaps he'll make
One day a Son unto himself – as he
Gave you a father – and if he so doth,
Mark me! that Son will be a Sacrifice.[68]

---

[68] Byron, *Cain*, Act 1, Scene 1, lines 125-166.

Lucifer's **inversion** of good and evil appeals to the angered Cain. And then Lucifer mentions the serpent:

> *Cain: Ah! didst* thou *tempt my mother?*

> *Lucifer: I tempt none,*
>   *Save with the truth: was not the Tree, the Tree*
>   *Of Knowledge? and was not the Tree of Life*
>   *Still fruitful? Did I bid her pluck them not?*
>   *Did I plant things prohibited within*
>   *The reach of beings innocent, and curious*
>   *By their own innocence? I would have made ye*
>   *Gods; and even He who thrust ye forth, so thrust ye*
>   *Because "Ye should not eat the fruits of life,*
>   *And become gods as we." Were those his words?*

> *Cain: They were, as I have heard from those who heard them,*
>   *In thunder.*

> *Lucifer: Then who was the Demon? He*
>   *Who would not let ye live, or he who would*
>   *Have made ye live for ever, in the joy*
>   *And power of Knowledge?*[69]

Byron's Lucifer continues to cast God as an evil tyrant who is the cause of human misery and death. Lucifer offers to show Cain the mysteries of life and death, and the two depart.

In the second act, Lucifer and Cain fly through the abyss of space, where the earth is but a "small blue circle" amidst the stars, and they

---

[69] Ibid, lines 196-209.

behold the glory of the universe. Next, they travel to the starless, dark realm of Hades, where they see the spirits of the creatures of Earth's past. Anguished about the futility of his mortality, Cain wishes to remain in Hades; he wants to die, but Lucifer reveals that he can only enter this realm through the Gates of Death. Cain summarizes their journey:

> *Thou hast shown me wonders: thou hast shown me those*
> *Mighty Pre-Adamites who walked the Earth*
> *Of which ours is the wreck: thou hast pointed out*
> *Myriads of starry worlds, of which our own*
> *Is the dim and remote companion, in*
> *Infinity of life: thou hast shown me shadows*
> *Of that existence with the dreaded name*
> *Which my sire brought us – Death; thou hast shown me much*[70]

At the end of the second act, Lucifer and Cain return to Earth, where Lucifer gives a defiant speech and declares the nature of good and evil to be independent of God:

> *Cain: Haughty Spirit!*
> *Thou speak'st it proudly; but thyself, though proud,*
> *Hast a superior.*

> *Lucifer: No! By Heaven, which he*
> *Holds, and the abyss, and the immensity*
> *Of worlds and life, which I hold with him – No!*
> *I have a Victor – true; but no superior.*
> *Homage he has from all – but none from me:*
> *I battle it against him, as I battled*

---

[70] Byron, *Cain*, Act 2, Scene 2, lines 358-365.

In highest Heaven – through all Eternity,
And the unfathomable gulphs of Hades,
And the interminable realms of space,
And the infinity of endless ages,
All, all, will I dispute! And world by world,
And star by star, and universe by universe,
Shall tremble in the balance, till the great
Conflict shall cease, if ever it shall cease,
Which it ne'er shall, till he or I be quenched!
And what can quench our immortality,
Or mutual and irrevocable hate?
He as a conqueror will call the conquered
Evil, *but what will be the* Good *he gives?*
Were I the victor, his *works would be deemed*
The only evil ones. And you, ye new
And scare-born mortals, what have been his gifts
To you already, in your little world?

Cain: But few; and some of those but bitter.

Lucifer: Back with me, then, to thine Earth, and try the rest
Of his celestial boons to you and yours.
Evil and Good are things in their own essence,
And not made good or evil by the Giver;
But if he gives you good – so call him; if
Evil springs from him, *do not name it* mine,
Till ye know better its true fount; and judge
Not by words, though of Spirits, but the fruits
Of your existence, such as it must be.
One good gift has the fatal apple given, –
Your reason *– let it not be overswayed*

72

By tyrannous threats to force you into faith
'Gainst all external sense and inward feeling:
Think and endure, – and form an inner world
In your own bosom – where the outward fails;
So shall you nearer be the spiritual
Nature, and war triumphant with your own.[71]

Lucifer's eternal conflict with God evokes the theme of **revolution**, and his defiant attitude reminds us of Satan from *Paradise Lost*.

In the final act, Abel insists on making a sacrifice to God with Cain. A pillar of flame consumes Abel's offering and carries it to Heaven, while a whirlwind destroys Cain's altar and scatters his offerings upon the earth. Cain tries to destroy Abel's altar; Abel stands in his way, and Cain strikes Abel, killing him. Before he dies, Abel asks God to forgive Cain.

Cain is cursed by Eve and shunned by Adam for his crime. The Angel of the Lord appears and curses Cain:

The voice of thy slain brother's blood cries out,
Even from the ground, unto the Lord! – Now art thou
Cursed from the Earth, which opened late her mouth
To drink thy brother's blood from thy rash hand.
Henceforth, when thou shalt till the ground, it shall not
Yield thee her strength; a fugitive shalt thou
Be from this day, and vagabond on Earth![72]

Cain begs for death, but the Angel refuses; it places a mark on Cain's brow to protect him from retribution and disappears. Cain and his

---

[71] Ibid, lines 424-466.

[72] Byron, *Cain*, Act 3, Scene 1, lines 470-476.

wife, Adah, leave with their son, Enoch, to wander the earth.

Ruben van Lujik emphasizes the importance of Byron's *Cain* to the genre of Romantic Satanism:

> *By the beginning of the 1820's, Godwin was all but forgotten, Blake was writing down his prophecies in utter obscurity, and Shelley's musings on Satan were virtually unnoticed or stacked away in as-yet-unpublished notebooks. The new Satan might have remained a minor footnote in literary history, had it not been for two almost diametrically opposed factors: Lord Byron, and conservative literary criticism.*[73]

That the Satanic themes in *Cain* were much more obvious than those found in *Manfred* was due to the political and literary challenges that emerged during the four years after *Manfred* was published. As an advocate for political reform, Byron was angered and upset by government oppression in his native England; as an author he was threatened and outraged by the censorship of the Blasphemous and Seditious Libels Act in 1820. Criticism from conservative authors also provoked Byron to lash out, as we will see in the next entry. Finally, Byron relocated to Pisa in 1821, where Shelley and his wife were living at the time, and it is likely that Byron was influenced by Shelley's own Satanic views.

Schock summarizes: "Lucifer's attacks on divine authority and the response they provoked in the first readers of *Cain* confirm that a major purpose of Byronic Satanism was to press against the limits of what could be published and tolerated in the last years of the Regency."[74] Not surprisingly, *Cain* was derided by critics for its blasphemous, anti-

---

[73] Lujik, *Children of Lucifer*, 71.

[74] Schock, *Romantic Satanism*, 8.

74

Christian tone.

Robert Southey: A Vision of Judgement

British poet Robert Southey (1774-1843) was not a Romantic Satanist, but he played an important role in the development of the genre, especially as a foil for Shelley and Byron.

Impressed with Robert Southey's poem *The Curse of Kehama,* Shelley and his new wife moved to Keswick in 1811, where Shelley sought guidance from the elder poet. However, their shared passion for writing could not overcome their stark political differences, and a month later Shelley moved on. When Southey was appointed British Poet Laureate by George III in 1813, Shelley and Byron branded Southey as a sell-out to the conservative government,[75] sparking an acrimonious relationship expressed in published poetry and prose.

Animosity between Southey and Byron led Byron to criticize Southey in a dedication to the elder poet in the poem *Don Juan* (1819):

> *I. Bob Southey! You 're a poet—Poet-laureate,*
> *And representative of all the race;*
> *Although 'tis true that you turn'd out a Tory at*
> *Last—yours has lately been a common case;*
> *And now, my Epic Renegade! what are ye at?*
> *With all the Lakers, in and out of place?*
> *A nest of tuneful persons, to my eye*
> *Like "four and twenty Blackbirds in a pye;*[76]

---

[75] As a political appointment, the Poet Laureate received a yearly salary from the King and was expected to write odes celebrating the King's birthday and the new year.

[76] Henry James Pye (1744-1813) was the Poet Laureate before Southey.

II. "Which pye being open'd they began to sing,"
(This old song and new simile holds good),
"A dainty dish to set before the King,"
Or Regent, who admires such kind of food;
And Coleridge, too, has lately taken wing,
But like a hawk encumber'd with his hood,
Explaining Metaphysics to the nation—
I wish he would explain his Explanation.

III. You, Bob! are rather insolent, you know,
At being disappointed in your wish
To supersede all warblers here below,
And be the only Blackbird in the dish;
And then you overstrain yourself, or so,
And tumble downward like the flying fish
Gasping on deck, because you soar too high, Bob,
And fall, for lack of moisture quite a-dry, Bob![77,78]

Southey responded to Byron's criticism in *A Vision of Judgement* (1822). Southey's poem commemorated recently deceased King George III, giving an account of his judgment and entry into Heaven. In the preface, Southey lashed out:

> *Men of diseased hearts and depraved imagination, who, forming*
> *a system of opinions to suit their own unhappy course of conduct,*
> *have rebelled against the holiest ordinances of human society,*

---

[77] According to Peter Cochran, a "dry-bob was Regency gentleman's slang for coition without emission."

[78] Lord Byron, *Don Juan*, Dedication, https://www.poetryfoundation.org/poems/43828/don-juan-dedication.

*and hating that revealed religion which, with all their efforts and
bravadoes, they are unable entirely to disbelieve, labour to make
others as miserable as themselves, by infecting them with a moral
virus that eats into the soul! The School that they have set up may
properly be called the Satanic School; for though their productions
breathe the spirit of Belial in their lascivious parts, and the spirit of
Moloch in those loathsome images of atrocities and horrors which
they delight to represent, they are more especially characterized by
a Satanic spirit of pride and audacious impiety, which still betrays
the wretched feeling of hopelessness wherewith it is allied.*[79]

Though not directly named, the preface alludes to Byron and Shelley.
According to Lujik, Southey's work is also the source of the terms
"Romantic Satanism" and "Literary Satanism."[80]

Byron retaliated with *The Vision of Judgment* (1822), a parody of
Southey's work. As you might have guessed, Byron's poem was much
more judgmental of George III. Byron's disdain for Southey comes
across clearly in the Preface:

*"It hath been wisely said, that 'One fool makes many;' and it hath
been poetically observed, 'That fools rush in where angels fear to
tread.'" – Pope.*

*If Mr. Southey had not rushed in where he had no business, and
where he never was before, and never will be again, the following
poem would not have been written. It is not impossible that it
may be as good as his own, seeing that it cannot, by any species*

---

[79] Robert Southey, *A Vision of Judgement*, Preface, Section III, 63. PDF. In Appendix
to Lord Byron, *A Vision of Judgment*, Peter Cochran, Ed., petercochran.files.word-
press.com/2009/03/the_vision_of_judgement3.pdf.

[80] Lujik, *Children of Lucifer*, 73.

of stupidity, natural or acquired, be worse. The gross flattery, the dull impudence, the renegado intolerance and impious cant of the poem by the author of Wat Tyler, are something so stupendous as to form the sublime of himself – containing the quintessence of his own attributes.

So much for his poem – a word on his preface. In this preface it has pleased the magnanimous Laureate to draw the picture of a supposed "Satanic School," that which he doth recommend to the notice of the legislature, thereby adding to his other laurels the ambition of those of an informer. If there exists anywhere, except in his imagination, such a school, is he not sufficiently armed against it by his own intense vanity?

. . . .

...with what conscience dare he call the attention of the laws to the publications of others, be they what they may? I say nothing of the cowardice of such a proceeding; its meanness speaks for itself; but I wish to touch upon the motive, which is neither more nor less, than that Mr.S. has been laughed at a little in some recent publications, as he was of yore in the "Anti-jacobin" by his present patrons. Hence all this "skimble scamble stuff" about "Satanic," and so forth. However, it is worthy of him – "Qualis ab incepto."[81]

If there is anything obnoxious to the political opinions of a portion of the public, in the following poem, they may thank Mr. Southey. He might have written hexameters, as he has written everything else, for aught that the writer cared – had they been upon another subject. But to attempt to canonise a Monarch, who, whatever were his household virtues, was neither a successful nor a patriotic king, – inasmuch as several years of his reign passed in war with America and Ireland, to say nothing of the

---

[81] Latin, "the same as from the beginning."

aggression upon France, – like all other exaggeration, necessarily begets opposition. In whatever manner he may be spoken of in this new "Vision," his public career will not be more favourably transmitted by history. Of his private virtues (although a little expensive to the nation) there can be no doubt.

With regard to the supernatural personages treated of, I can only say that I know as much about them, and (as an honest man) have a better right to talk of them than Robert Southey. I have also treated them more tolerantly. The way in which that poor insane creature, the Laureate, deals about his judgements in the next world, is like his own judgement in this. If it was not completely ludicrous, it would be something worse. I don't think that there is much more to say at present.[82]

Byron's scathing parody humiliated Southey; critic Geoffrey Carnall wrote, "Southey's reputation has never recovered from Byron's ridicule."[83]

---

[82] Lord Byron, *A Vision of Judgment*, Preface, Peter Cochran, Ed., 2-3, PDF, petercochran.files.wordpress.com/2009/03/the_vision_of_judgement3.pdf.

[83] Quoted from Wikipedia, *The Vision of Judgment*, https://en.wikipedia.org/wiki/The_Vision_of_Judgment#cite_note-1.

Chapter Five:
The French Romantic Satanists

The three great English poets of Romantic Satanism died in the 1820's. Blake lived to be almost seventy, but the lives of Shelley and Byron were both cut tragically short by accident and illness. That same decade saw the advent of Romantic Satanism in France.

Alfred de Vigny: Eloa

First among the French Romantic Satanists was poet, novelist, and playwright Alfred de Vigny (1797-1863). The young Vigny became a second lieutenant in the elite King's Guard after the Bourbon monarchy was restored in 1814, but he found peacetime service in the military boring and turned his attention to literary pursuits. He published his first poem, *Le Bal*, in 1820, and his first novel, *Cinq-Mars*, in 1826, and translated three of Shakespeare's plays into French by 1829. At the end of the decade Vigny was regarded as one of the leading figures of the Romantic movement in France, eclipsed only by Victor Hugo.

Vigny's contribution to Romantic Satanism was the poem *Eloa, or the Sister of the Angels* (1824). In the first canto, Birth, we witness the birth of the angel Eloa from a tear shed by Jesus over the corpse of Lazarus:

O holy tear given to friendship!
You were not abandoned to the winds!
A diamond urn, with Seraphim leaning over it,
Invisible to mortals, received it softly;
Like a marvel, astonishing even to the Heavens,
Carried you sparkling to the feet of the Eternal.
A favorable look from the ever-open eye
Touched the ineffable gift and caused it to shine,
And the Holy Spirit, pouring forth his power upon her,
Gave soul and life to the divine essence.
Just as the incense, which burns in the sun's rays,
Changes into pure fire, a brilliant cherry-red,
So was a white and growing form
Seen to go up from the heart of the dazzling urn.
A voice was heard which said: "Eloa!"
And the Angel appeared and said: "Here am I!"

All adorned in the sight of the watching Heavens
She marched towards God like a bride to the Temple,
Her beauteous brow, serene and pure like a beautiful lily,
Raised the folds of an azure veil;
Her hair, parted as with blond sprays,
Lost in the mists of the air their soft waves,
Just as a wandering comet is seen in the skies,
Blending its gracious rays in the bosom of the night;
A rose in the glimmers of the morning dawn
Lacks the virginal blush of its fresh tint;
And the moon, brightening the dense woods
Fails to attain the sweetness of even one of its sweet looks.
Her wings were of silver; under a pale robe
Her white foot by turns disclosed and hid itself,

And her heaving breast, scarce perceived,
Raised the contours of the heavenly film.
She was both, a woman and a charming Angel;
For the spirit people, a loving family,
Near us, for us, prays and watches ever,
Uniting pure essences in holy acts of love.[84]

The angels warn Eloa about Lucifer:

One day the inhabitants of the immortal empire,
Who once were careless, united to counsel her:
"Eloa," they said, "Oh, be very careful:
An angel can fall: the most beautiful of us all
Is here no longer. Yet in his initial virtue
He was called the light-bearer;
For he carried love and life in every place,
He carried God's orders to the stars,
The Earth consecrated his matchless beauty
By calling the morning star Lucifer,
A radiant diamond which the Sun had placed
On his vermilion brow amidst his golden hair.
Yet now, 'tis said, he is bereft of diadem,
He groans, he is alone, none love him,
Of crime the blackness weighs upon his eyes,
No longer does he know the tongue of Heaven,
And death resides in the words of his mouth.
He burns what he sees, he withers what he touches,

---

[84] Alfred de Vigny, *Eloa, or the Sister of the Angels*, First Canto, trans. Alan de Corré, https://minds.wisconsin.edu/bitstream/handle/1793/61400/eloaweb.html?sequence=1.

He senses not evil or good deeds;
Joyless is he at the ills which he has done.
Heaven where once he lived is troubled by his memory,
No angel will dare tell you his story,
No Saint would dare ever to utter his name.
They thought that Eloa would curse him; but no,
Fear did not change at all her untroubled face,
And this was an alarming omen for Heaven.
Not to tremble was her first impulse,
But rather to draw near as it were to help;
Sadness appeared on her icy lip
As soon as a sad thought offered itself;
She learned to dream, and her innocent face
Fell blushing at this unknown trouble.
A tear shone on her eyelid.
Happy the heart whose first tear is thus shed![85]

Eloa falls in love with this fallen angel and seeks him out, descending to "the bottom of the lowest Heavens" and into the void.

In the second canto, The Seduction, the fallen angel introduces himself to Eloa, then tempts her:

I am he who is loved and is not known.
On man I have founded my fiery empire
In the desires of the heart, in the dreams of the soul,
In the ties of the bodies, mysterious attractions,
In the treasures of the blood, in the looks of the eyes.
I am he who makes the wife speak in her dreams;
The happy young girl learns happy lies;

---

[85] Vigny, *Eloa*, First Canto.

I give her nights which console her days;
I am the secret King of secret loves.
I unite hearts, break strong chains,
As the butterfly on its dusty wings
Brings to the bursting lawns a parade of flowers,
Making love to them without perils and tears.
I have taken from the Creator his weak creature;
In his despite, we have carved up Nature:
I let him, proud of the noise of cherry-red day,
Hide the golden stars 'neath the sliver of a Sun;
But I am the silent shadow, giving the earth
The joys of eventide and the good things of the mystery.

Have you come with several Angels of Heaven
To admire the delicious course of my nights?
Have you seen their treasures? Do you know what marvels
Attend the evenings of the dark Angels?
. . . . .
Here for your inspection are the 'Evildoer's' works;
This accusèd rogue in truth is a Consoler.
He bewails the slave, and takes him from his lord,
Saves him lovingly from the sorrows of his state,
And burièd himself in the common ill,
Grants him a little charm—and oft nepenthe.[86]

In the third canto, The Fall, the fallen angel almost falls in love with Eloa… but he cannot:

Oh, how sad the love of sin! How dark the desires of evil!

---

[86] Vigny, *Eloa*, Second Canto.

How immense the thoughts of knowledge!
How came I to know your senseless ardor?
Cursed be the time that I stood up to God;
Oh, the simplicity of heart to which I bade adieu!
I tremble before you, yet I adore you still;
I am less the criminal, since I still love you:
But into my withered heart you will come nevermore!
I'm far from what I was, yea, so many steps I've ta'en
And now so great the distance from myself to me
That I can grasp no longer what innocence has to say.
I suffer, and my spirit, battered by evil,
No longer can attain such heights of virtue.
What has become of you, O peaceful, heavenly days
When, first among the modest Angels, I went forth
To genuflect before the ancient Law,
And thought of nothing beyond faith?
Eternity opened before me like a feast,
With flowers in my hands, a diadem on my head,
I smiled, I was...Perhaps I could have loved!"
The Tempter himself was almost charmed;
He had forgot his wiles and his victim,
And for a moment he drew back from his crime.
Quite low he repeated, with his brow in his hands:
"O human tears, would that I had known you!"[87]

Eloa gives into seduction:

Some Angels were going to drag some worlds to Chaos.
Passing with terror through these deep plains,

---

[87] Vigny, *Eloa*, Third Canto.

While fulfiling the messages of God,
They saw a cloud of fire fall.
Cries of pain, cruel responses,
Mixed together in the flame to the flapping of wings.

"Where are you taking me, beautiful Angel?" "Come on."
"How sad is your voice, and somber your talk!
Is not Eloa removing your chain?
I thought I had saved you." "No, it is I who am dragging you off."
"If we are together, I don't care where it is!
Call me then your Sister or your God!"
"I carry off my slave, I have my victim."
"You seemed so good! Oh, what have I done?" "A crime."
"Will you at least be happier, are you content?"
"Sadder than ever." "Who are you, then?" "Satan."[88]

At the end of the poem the fallen angel reveals his true name: Satan!

Vigny's poem employs the theme of **inversion** by making the fallen angel more desirable than the inhabitants of Heaven. According to Lujik, the poem was very popular:

Eloa *enjoyed considerable popularity with the French public. Fashionable would-be Eloas wrote love letters comparing their beloved to Satan, and Theophile Gautier remarked in a satirical sketch that he considered himself extraordinarily lucky to be blessed with a natural pale and olive-colored complexion, as this assured him of favor with the ladies because of his likeness to the archdemon.*[89]

---

[88] Ibid.

[89] Lujik, *Children of Lucifer*, 75.

Alphonse Louis Constant: The Bible of Liberty

French Deacon, author, and artist Alphonse Louis Constant (1810-1875) is better known by his esoteric nom de plume, Eliphas Levi. However, before he became the master of occultism, Constant was politically active as an advocate of Christian Socialism, a blend of religious and political philosophy that sought to establish a socialist utopia based on the teachings of Jesus.

Constant's ideas about Satan were significantly different than those of the traditional Catholic Church. In the early 1830's, while still in seminary, Constant rejected the doctrine of eternal damnation, and believed that Hell, the traditional domain of Satan, did not exist. Constant also believed in the millenarian prophecies of theologian Joachim of Fiore, who divided history into three epochs ruled by a member of the Christian Trinity. The first two epochs having already occurred, believers awaited the Age of the Paraclete (Holy Spirit), which would bring people into direct contact with God and create a Christian utopia upon Earth. Many people (Constant among them) believed that the Age of Revolution would bring about the changes necessary for the Age of the Paraclete to begin.

In 1841, Constant published *The Bible of Liberty*, a revolutionary and socialist reinterpretation of the Scriptures. In *The Bible of Liberty*, Constant makes a distinction between Lucifer and Satan:

> *The angel of despotism is the angel of murder and debauchery; he hates the woman and pursues her with implacable rage, but the woman will crush his head.*
>
> *The spirit of evil is not Lucifer, the glorious rebel; it is Satan, the angel of domination and slavery.*
>
> *It is Satan who tempts the world, and it is Lucifer who saves it by raising it against Satan.*

Satan is the father of the law; Lucifer is the father of grace.
Despotism is death; and freedom is life.
Despotism is the flesh; and freedom is the spirit.
Despotism is hell; and freedom is heaven.[90]

The Bible of Liberty dedicates an entire chapter to Lucifer, defined as

...the angel of light, or otherwise of science. He was worthy of the
centuries of ignorance that made him the prince of demons.[91]

Constant believed mankind would be saved if Lucifer reconciled with
God and was accepted back into Heaven. Thus, Constant's Lucifer is
an agent of both **revolution** and **redemption**.

The angel of liberty was born before dawn, and God called it the
morning star.
    Glory to you, o Lucifer, because, being the most sublime of all
intelligences, you have been able to believe yourself the equal of
God!
    And you fell like lightning, from the sky where the sun drowned
you in the light, to furrow with your own rays the dark and majestic
sky of the night.
    You shine when the sun goes down, and your sparkling gaze
precedes the sunrise.
    And when the day has conquered the darkness, you will not be
extinguished, lonely star; but you will rush into the sun, whose

---

[90] Alphonse Louis Constant, *The Bible of Liberty*, (Daath Gnosis Publishing, 2012), 36, Chapter VIII: "The Fall of the Angels." Translation cleaned up by Michael Osiris Snuffin.

[91] Constant, *The Bible of Liberty*, footnote to p.30, Chapter VI: "Lucifer."

rays will never blot out your splendor.

You will come back victorious and you will be around God as a diadem of glory; you will shine on his heart like a diamond.

The Father will arm you with his lightning; the Son will give you a scepter surmounted by a cross; and the Spirit, under the figure of a young virgin with a sweet smile, will put the first kiss of her love on your scarred forehead!

And you will be like the triumphant warrior who returns to the home of his father.

And you will be called the light of the world, beautiful angel of freedom!

No, you are not the spirit of evil, generous spirit of revolt and noble pride!

Evil is nothingness, it is the deprivation of good, and good is freedom!

For freedom is the daughter of intelligence and the mother of love.

Perish all the joys of slaves! they can only perpetuate their shame! but glory will triumph exiled in the eternal cry of the outcast.

He fought against God and he defeated him; for it is to be victorious to have fought against him.

God can only be defeated by his equal, and his equal is himself.

O Lucifer! you came out of the bosom of God, and God called you back to him.

You are the breath of his mouth and the aspiration of his heart.

You did not listen because you understood; and you did not obey because you loved.

Glory to you, spirit of intelligence and love! because, as Christ suffered the torment of the cross, you endured the torment of hell! the world cursed you as it cursed him, and like him you were counted among the dead; but behold, you are risen again, immortal redeemer of the angels!

*And Christ, who is still crowned with thorns in the heaven where
he reigns, will receive from your hands a crown of gold.*

*For the gold has been purified by the flames, and the flames are
eternal as the hearth of love that lights them.*

*The spirit of love is a furnace that burns and consumes hatred;
it is a lake of fire, always motionless and always active.*

*And hell and death have been thrown into this lake of fire, and
they will be no more.*[92]

The Bible of Liberty was seized by the authorities and Constant was tried
and convicted of sedition and blasphemy, earning him a prison sentence
of eleven months. Constant was imprisoned twice more for writing
seditious material, but drifted away from political activism after the
Revolution of 1848.

In the 1850's Constant reinvented himself as the occultist Eliphas Levi,
publishing books that drew popular interest to the Occult Sciences (such
as astrology, alchemy, Kabala, and tarot cards) and sparking the French
occult revival in the last part of the 19th century. In his magnum opus,
Dogma and Ritual of High Magic (1856), Levi discards Satan altogether:

*Let us say aloud, to combat against the remains of Manichaeism
which still arise in our time among Christians, that Satan as a
superior personality and as a power does not exist. Satan is the
personification of all errors, of all perversity, and in consequences
of all weakness. If God can be defined as he who necessarily
exists, can we not define his antagonist and his enemy as he who*

---

[92] Constant, *The Bible of Liberty*, 30-32, Chapter VI: "Lucifer."

necessarily does not exist?[93]

George Sand: Consuelo

French novelist George Sand (1804-1876) stands with Honore de Balzac and Victor Hugo as one of the greatest and most popular French novelists of the 19th century. She was noted for her disregard of gender norms of the time, using a male pseudonym, wearing masculine clothing (pants) and smoking in public. Sand was a prolific writer who was also known for her many love affairs, including one with composer Frederic Chopin.

Sand published the novel *Consuelo* serially between 1842-43. It tells the story of a young Romani woman in Venice who escapes poverty and finds fame as an opera singer. Her beautiful voice and her success attract many suitors, including the eccentric Count Albert Rudolstadt, with whom she falls in love. Consuelo, torn between her stage career and the man she loves, finally marries Count Albert shortly before he dies and inherits his fortune and title.

At one point in the novel Consuelo has a vision of Satan, who tells her:

> *I am not the demon. I am the archangel of legitimate rebellion and the patron of the great struggles. Like Christ, I am the god of the poor, the weak, and the oppressed....O people! Don't you recognize him who has spoken to you in the secrecy of your heart since you have existed, he who has given you solace in all your distress, telling you: seek happiness, don't give up on it! You have*

---

[93] Eliphas Levi, *Dogma and Ritual of High Magic*, trans. John Michael Greer and Mark Anthony Mikituk, (New York, TarcherPerigee, 2017), 318, Chapter VI: "Lucifer."

a right to happiness; demand it, and you will have it![94]

The vision ends with Consuelo falling to her knees in front of Satan.[95] The novel uses the themes of **revolution** and **inversion** to make positive connections between Consuelo and the Devil.

According to Faxneld, Consuelo herself is sometimes compared to the Devil:

> *When she has performed an aria from Galuppi's 1755 opera* La Diavolessa, *her teacher is so impressed that he exclaims "It is you who are Satan himself!" When she has later helped him with a musical composition he is working on, he says "You are the Devil! I always thought that you were the Devil!" She answers: "a kindly Devil, believe me, Master." When she spurns the advances of a wicked baron, he asks himself "what manner of she-devil is this?" A self-assertive woman turning down a man hence becomes a "diablesse", and a woman with sufficient musical talent to assist her teacher in composing music is also diabolical.*[96]

Flora Tristan: The Emancipation of Woman

Flora Tristan (1803-1844) was a French feminist and socialist activist. She was the first person to connect the oppression of workers with the oppression of women, and she believed that liberating both groups would lead to a socialist utopia. Tristan wrote a number of influential books, including *Peregrinations of a Pariah* (1838), *Promenades in London* (1840), and *The Workers' Union* (1843). She died while on a tour of

---

[94] Lujik, *Children of Lucifer*, 121.

[95] Faxneld, *Satanic Feminism*, 91-92.

[96] Ibid, 92.

France, working to encourage and empower male and female activists to join a national Worker's Union.

Her final book, *The Emancipation of Woman*, was completed from her notes and published by her friend and spiritual mentor, Alphonse Louis Constant. There are questions as to how much influence Constant had on this work. Both authors use the themes of **revolution** and **redemption** in their **reinterpretation** of Satanic mythology. It is only in Tristan's work, however, that Satan is redeemed by a female angel.

GENIUS AND LOVE

A sacred instinct guides all peoples unconsciously in the choice and exhibition of their symbols.

Thus, in our times, at the place where despotism once located its dungeons, we raised a pillar to liberty, and, on the top of this pillar shines the angel of light, the young and glorious Lucifer![97]

Lucifer, the angel of genius and science who was relegated to hell's throne by medieval superstition, but now, freed by human conscience, mounts triumphantly up to heaven, with a star on his forehead, holding in his right hand an unquenchable torch.

Thus Holy Spirit has now gained, like the Father and Son, a human form offered to humanity; the symbolic dove folds its white wings out of sight.

The spirit of intelligence and love is now manifest through the young, smiling features of Lucifer! Intelligence has been freed: he rises victoriously from the abyss of reprobation, hand in hand with the gracious angel of Love, who had shared in his exile.

For Lucifer was not alone in his fall: he had brought a friend.

---

[97] Tristan here describes the July Column in the Place de la Bastille, where Auguste Dumont's Génie de la Liberté (Spirit of Freedom) stands atop a gilded globe; the figure resembles Lucifer.

When the Father of beings executed his words: Let there be light! *His glance was lighted up with glory.*

The rays of his diadem were detached from his forehead and fell around him like a golden rain.

Then each drop of light took a form unknown to heaven, and became an angel.

But a finer and greater spirit than the rest was born from the visage itself, and from the resplendent smile of God.

All the spirits bowed down at birth; that one alone remained standing, and he was sad, for in the beaming of the visage of God that he was made of, there was a burst of liberty and a spark of power.

God then looked at this fine angel with the jealous love that all mothers would eventually know, and said to him: Why are you sad?

—Because I see your glory which forces me to worship you, responded Lucifer, and my love for you is too noble ever to be enslaved!

Immediately the Lord took off his azure, star-studded cloak, and held it between his face and that of the beloved angel. A dark night enveloped nature at its birth, and the star that scintillated on the forehead of Lucifer, was the only thing shining now, and it showed him the depths of his solitude. The angel of light cried; he rose triumphantly, eyes bathed in tears; he would be miserable, but he would be free!

Near him, on an arid and desolate boulder—one of the bones of the old chaos laid bare by these recent convulsions—was seated another angel who looked at him, and who cried while looking on him with a pain-filled smile.

"Who are you?" the rebel angel asked.

"I am your brother Ariel, or rather, to borrow a word from human

language, I am your sister, *O Lucifer!*

"You are the angel of Genius, and I am the genius of Love. You came out from God's forehead by his glance, as an effusion of his greatness, while I came from his heart as a transmission of his smile, as a whisper from his infinite love.

"I cannot live without you, so I came into your exile to be lost with you, suffer with you, and to save myself along with you."

"Oh, thank you!" returned Lucifer, as he laid his first kiss on the forehead of Ariel, saying:

"Sister, a great work is given to us. We must liberate the creatures of God by intelligence and love, by making them stronger than fear and pain. Let us fashion a hell in order to ennoble the path to heaven."

From then on the human race would be split in two: the troop of the timid, and the phalanx of the brave: Those afraid to lose an unearned inheritance and who let their liberty lie dormant, and those who take liberty alone for their inheritance, renouncing all else.

Yet, I tell you truly that, if God has pity on the former, he will love the latter with all his love, because liberty is the finest and noblest of his gifts.

Here are the signs by which he will recognize them:

They are those in whom love is more powerful than any fear;

Those who disdain evil and have no fear of hell;

Those who do good for its own sake, and not by way of pleasing or obeying men;

In the end, those who will find reprobation glorious so long as they are approved by their own spirit and heart, for they will be persecuted by servile spirits, and people will think they shame them by calling them, as they have done with me, reprobates and pariahs!

A thunderclap followed this word of the greatest of angels; and he, like a herald who raises the trumpet and senses the battle from afar, he proudly raises his head, holds Ariel close to his chest, and, puffed up with courage, looks at heaven with a tranquil pride and seems to become drunk on the thunder.

As to Ariel, she did not hear the thunder, they did not notice the lightning tearing the dark night; for her face, full of ecstasy, was lost gazing into Lucifer's eyes.[98]

Like Milton's Satan, Tristan's Lucifer chooses liberty in Hell over servitude in Heaven. But here, the angel of intelligence is redeemed by the angel of love, and together they bring liberty to the human race.

Charles Baudelaire: The Flowers of Evil

French poet Charles Baudelaire (1821-1867) was very active in the artistic and literary circles of the mid-19th century, rubbing elbows with other notables such as Victor Hugo, Franz Liszt, and Honore de Balzac. His career in literature was not supported by his wealthy family, and his extravagant lifestyle swallowed up inheritances and gifts. Like Alphonse Louis Constant, Baudelaire was a political radical in his youth who drifted away from politics after the Revolution of 1848.

The Flowers of Evil (1857) was Baudelaire's first published collection of poems. It included the poem "Litany to Satan." Shortly after it went on sale, copies of the book were seized, and Baudelaire and his publisher were charged with committing an offense against public morals. Baudelaire defended his work in court, and his friends in the literary world supported him in print. In the end, Baudelaire was fined

[98] Flora Tristan, *The Emancipation of Woman*, trans. Kirk Watson, Kindle.

300 francs, six poems were suppressed,[99] and Baudelaire gained more fame and notoriety in France.

The "Litany to Satan" is based on a Catholic prayer known as the *Miserere* (Latin for "have mercy"). Baudelaire, who was raised in the Catholic Church, would have been familiar with this prayer. Baudelaire employs the theme of **inversion**, adoring and asking for mercy from Satan:

Litany to Satan

O grandest of the Angels, and most wise,
   O fallen God, fate-driven from the skies,
   Satan, at last take pity on our pain.

O first of exiles who endurest wrong,
   Yet growest, in thy hatred, still more strong,
   Satan, at last take pity on our pain!

O subterranean King, omniscient,
   Healer of man's immortal discontent,
   Satan, at last take pity on our pain.

To lepers and to outcasts thou dost show
   That Passion is the Paradise below.
   Satan, at last take pity on our pain.

Thou by thy mistress Death hast given to man
   Hope, the imperishable courtesan.
   Satan, at last take pity on our pain.

---

[99] The six scandalous poems were all about lurid sex and lesbians, not Satan.

Thou givest to the Guilty their calm mien
Which damns the crowd around the guillotine
Satan, at last take pity on our pain.

Thou knowest the corners of the jealous Earth
Where God has hidden jewels of great worth.
Satan, at last take pity on our pain.

Thou dost discover by mysterious signs
Where sleep the buried people of the mines.
Satan, at last take pity on our pain.

Thou stretchest forth a saving hand to keep
Such men as roam upon the roofs in sleep.
Satan, at last take pity on our pain.

Thy power can make the halting Drunkard's feet
Avoid the peril of the surging street.
Satan, at last take pity on our pain.

Thou, to console our helplessness, didst plot
The cunning use of powder and of shot.
Satan, at last take pity on our pain.

Thy awful name is written as with pitch
On the unrelenting foreheads of the rich.
Satan, at last take pity on our pain.

In strange and hidden places thou dost move
Where women cry for torture in their love.
Satan, at last take pity on our pain.

Father of those whom God's tempestuous ire
Has flung from Paradise with sword and fire,
Satan, at last take pity on our pain.

Prayer
Satan, to thee be praise upon the Height
Where thou wast king of old, and in the night
Of Hell, where thou dost dream on silently.
Grant that one day beneath the Knowledge-tree,
When it shoots forth to grace thy royal brow,
My soul may sit, that cries upon thee now.[100]

Pierre-Joseph Proudhon: On Justice in Revolution and Church

French politician and philosopher Pierre-Joseph Proudhon (1809-1865) is perhaps best known as the father of anarchism. He was the first person to call himself an anarchist, and he wrote a number of influential books on the subject. He is best known for his first publication, *What is Property?*, and the answer to the title question contained therein, "property is theft," which became Proudhon's slogan.

Proudhon used Satan to provoke and scandalize his audience. In *The System of Economic Contradictions* (1847), Proudhon examined and denied what he called "the hypothesis of a God":

> *The sins which we ask you to forgive, you caused us to commit;*
> *the traps from which we implore you to deliver us, you set for us;*

---

[100] Charles Baudelaire, "Litany to Satan," trans. James Elroy Flecker, in *The Collected Poems of James Elroy Flecker* (New York, Doubleday, Page & Co, 1916), 42-44, https://en.wikisource.org/wiki/The_collected_poems_of_James_Elroy_Flecker/Litany_to_Satan.

and the Satan who besets us is yourself.

You triumphed, and no one dared to contradict you, when, after having tormented in his body and in his soul the righteous Job, a type of our humanity, you insulted his candid piety, his prudent and respectful ignorance. We were as naught before your invisible majesty, to whom we gave the sky for a canopy and the earth for a footstool. And now here you are dethroned and broken. Your name, so long the last word of the savant, the sanction of the judge, the force of the prince, the hope of the poor, the refuge of the repentant sinner, — this incommunicable name, I say, henceforth an object of contempt and curses, shall be a hissing among men. For God is stupidity and cowardice; God is hypocrisy and falsehood; God is tyranny and misery; God is evil. As long as humanity shall bend before an altar, humanity, the slave of kings and priests, will be condemned; as long as one man, in the name of God, shall receive the oath of another man, society will be founded on perjury; peace and love will be banished from among mortals. God, take yourself away! for, from this day forth, cured of your fear and become wise, I swear, with hand extended to heaven, that you are only the tormentor of my reason, the spectre of my conscience.

I deny, therefore, the supremacy of God over humanity; I reject his providential government, the non-existence of which is sufficiently established by the metaphysical and economical hallucinations of humanity, — in a word, by the martyrdom of our race; I decline the jurisdiction of the Supreme Being over man; I take away his titles of father, king, judge, good, merciful, pitiful, helpful, rewarding, and avenging. All these attributes, of which the idea of Providence is made up, are but a caricature of humanity, irreconcilable with the autonomy of civilization, and contradicted, moreover, by the history of its aberrations and catastrophes.[101]

Proudhon's **inversion** casts the Christian God as an evil tyrant. His later works glorify Satan as a symbol of liberty:

> *Liberty, which you cannot deny without destroying yourself, which you cannot affirm without destroying yourself still, you dread it as the Sphinx dreaded Oedipus: it came, and the riddle of the Church was answered; Christianity is no longer anything other than an episode in the mythology of the human race. Liberty, symbolized by the story of the Temptation, is your Antichrist; liberty, for you, is the Devil.*
>
> *Come, Satan, come, slandered by priests and kings! Let me embrace you, let me clutch you to my breast! I have known you for a long time, and you know me as well. Your works, oh blessed of my heart, are not always beautiful or good; but you alone give sense to the universe and prevent it from being absurd. What would justice be without you? An instinct. Reason? A routine. Man? A beast. You alone prompt labor and render it fertile; you ennoble wealth, serve as an excuse for authority, put the seal on virtue. Hope still, proscript! I have at your service only a pen, but it is worth millions of ballots. And I wish only to ask when the days sung of by the poet will return:*
>
> *You crossed gothic ruins;*
> *Our defenders pressed at your heels;*
> *Flowers rained down, and modest virgins*

---

[101] Pierre Joseph Proudhon, *The System of Economic Contradictions*, Chapter VIII, "Of the Responsibility of Man and Of God, Under the Law of Contradiction, Or a Solution of the Problem of Providence," trans. Benjamin R. Tucker (1888), https://theanarchistlibrary.org/library/pierre-joseph-proudhon-system-of-economical-contradictions-or-the-philosophy-of-poverty.

Mingled their songs with the war-hymn.
All stirred, and armed themselves for the defense;
All were proud, above all the poor.
Ah! Give back to me the days of my childhood,
Goddess of Liberty![102]

The poetic verses at the end of this quote became known as Proudhon's "Hymn to Satan," adding a demonic edge to a man already notorious in his time for his numerous attacks on principles of property and government. His convictions were not without consequences. Proudhon was arrested in 1849 and imprisoned for three years for attacking newly-elected President Louis Napoleon Bonaparte as an enemy of democracy and socialism, but his prophecy was fulfilled two years later when Napoleon seized power and declared himself Emperor.

Victor Hugo: The End of Satan

Victor Hugo (1802-1885) is one of the greatest French writers, best known for the classic novels *The Hunchback of Notre-Dame* (1831) and *Les Misérables* (1862) and his many celebrated collections of poetry.

Stunned by the death of Lord Byron in 1824, the young Hugo wrote an obituary in *La Muse Francaise* titled "On George Gordon, Lord Byron" that alludes to Southey's Satanic school:

Two schools have formed themselves within its breast, representing the double situation in which our political troubles have left thinking people: resignation or despair....The first sees everything

---

[102] Pierre Joseph Proudhon, *On Justice in Revolution and Church*, Eighth Study: "Conscience and Freedom," trans. Shawn P. Wilbur (2018),
   https://www.libertarian-labyrinth.org/working-translations/proudhon-justice-eighth-study/.

from up in heaven; the other, from the bottom of the pit....The
first, in sum, resembles Immanuel, mild and strong, coursing over
his kingdom on a chariot of lightning and light; the other is that
superb Satan who swept with him a such a number of stars when
he was thrown out of heaven.[103]

After being elected to the venerable Académie française in 1841, Hugo became involved in politics, known as an advocate for the working class and for his opposition to the death penalty. When Napoleon III seized power in a coup d'état in 1951, Hugo condemned him as a traitor to France. Feeling that he and his family were in danger, Hugo went into self-imposed exile until the Second Empire ended in 1870.

Hugo worked on the poem *The End of Satan* between 1854 and 1862, but never completed it; it was published in 1886, a year after his death. The poem is a **reinterpretation** of the fall of Satan and a **redemption** of Satan within the context of the Old Testament, the Gospel of Jesus Christ, and the French Revolution.

The poem begins with Satan falling into a terrifying abyss of darkness. Only a feather from his wings escapes the abyss:

> *Now, near the heavens, at the edge of the pit where nothing*
>   *Changes, a pure, white feather, which had escaped from the*
>   *Wings of the archangel, sat fluttering, precariously.*
>   *The angel before whom a dazzling dawn was breaking,*
>   *Saw it, gathered it up, and said, his eyes resting on the sublime*
> *sky:*
>   *—Lord, should the feather also go into the abyss?—*
>   *God, absorbed in Being and in Life, turned,*

---

[103] Quoted in Lujik, *Children of Lucifer*, 75.

And said:—Do not cast down that which is not fallen.[104]

Then Hugo describes the biblical story of Noah and the flood, the destruction of all evil life upon the earth, and the re-establishment of evil after the waters recede. Nimrod appears as the embodiment of War, declaring himself the ancestor of the Titans of Greek mythology and of Satan. Meanwhile, the angel of Liberty is born from the white feather:

Suddenly a light beam from His prodigious eye,
    Which formed the world from daylight, fell upon it.
    Under this shaft of soft and supernatural light,
    The feather quivered, shone, pulsated, grew,
    Took shape, came alive, and seemed
    A splendor transformed into a woman.
    With the mysterious shifting of a soul,
    She arose, and, standing erect,
    Lit infinity with her innocent smile.
    And the angels, trembling with love, beheld her.
    The twin cherubs clinging one to the other,
    The constellations of morning and evening,
    The Virtues, the Spirits, leaned forward to see
    This sister born of hell and of paradise.
    Never had the sacred heavens, amidst murmurs
    And whispers, contemplated a being more sublime.
    Seeing her so proud and so pure,
    They hesitated between calling her eagle or virgin.
    Her face, melding flame with brilliance,

---

[104]Victor Hugo, *God and The End of Satan*, R.G. Skinner, Tr., (Chicago, Swan Isle Press 2014), 199.

Blazed, defying the engulfing abyss;
It was, under a charming brow,
The glance of lightning with the eye of Dawn.

The archangel of the sun, gilded by a celestial fire,
Said:—O Lord, what shall we call this angel?

Then, in the absolute where this Being dwells,
One heard emerge from the depths of the Logos,
This Word which suddenly made a star blossom
Upon the brow of the magnificent, young angel,
Still half-formed and floating in the vast light:—Liberty.[105]

In the next part, Hugo presents his own stark interpretation of the life of Jesus, his betrayal and crucifixion. His account then moves forward 1800 years, to the French Revolution, where justice is corrupted and the words of Jesus forgotten:

Oh! Since this is the way things are to be,
Because the world always slays her prophets,
What are we to think and believe, O vast Heaven?
The priest is factious towards the truth;
All cults, blowing out Hell from their nostrils,
Chew bones infused with their doctrines;
All have proclaimed themselves true on pain of death;
No altar on earth, alas, is guiltless.
Everywhere the false gods have left their scars
On nature, the supreme and holy womb;
Everywhere Man is wicked, mean-hearted and proud-eyed,

---

[105] Hugo, *The End of Satan*, 217-219.

And deserves mighty strikes of lightning;
In his hands every deity degenerates
Into an idol, and becomes also deserving of thunderbolts.
So, who is wrong? Who is right? Who knows the answer?
Every day God seems to be further engulfed
In the soundless and fatal depths of empty space;
The Zend[106] is dark; the Talmud pale;
One wonders what the temples, and the gods sensed there,
Prefer to see smoking: incense, or blood?
In every church murder has seeped into its flagstones;
Pulpits create needless scandals down below, and
Thunderbolts cast needless lightning up above;
How one must act and what one must believe, alas!
Are almost always in conflict and rarely in accord.
The deep chasm opens; a dogma is a rope hanging in
The vast shadow, and vanishing into the pit.

Thus did Jesus die; and the people, dismayed,
Have since felt that the Unknown, itself,
Had appeared before them embodied in this Supreme Being,
And that his gospel was as Heaven.
Golgotha, sinister and pestilential,
Seems to be the deformed tumor of the abyss;
Wild beast, it arises from the unutterable bosom of corruption;
And the abyss casts its palest lightning on this place
Where sinister religion murdered God.[107]

In the last part of the poem, Satan recounts how his oppression drove

---

[106] The Zend Avesta contains the religious texts of Zoroastrianism.

[107] Hugo, *The End of Satan*, 303-305.

him to sow evil in the world, and expresses his desire to escape the misery of the abyss of Hell. The angel of Liberty seeks him out, descends into the abyss, and redeems Satan:

> Satan under his vault—
> *I draw myself up, marked by the appalling feature*
> *(The last stage of the horror!)—Love hates me.*
>
> *A Voice across the Infinite*
> *No, I do not hate you*
> ....
> *We are related through an angel; what she did affects you.*
> *Man, enchained by you, by her is freed.*
> *O Satan, you need only say: I shall live!*
> *Come, the destroyed prison abolishes Hell!*
> *Come, the angel Liberty is both your daughter and mine.*
> *This sublime fatherhood unites us.*
> *The archangel again lives, and the devil is no more;*
> *I efface the sinister night, and nothing of it remains.*
> *Satan is dead, be reborn, O celestial Lucifer,*
> *Come, arise out of the darkness with the dawn on your brow!*[108]

Hugo's "destroyed prison" was the Bastille, and it was the French Revolution that gave birth to the angel of Liberty, who liberated Satan and transformed him back into Lucifer, and who freed humanity from "sinister religion."

---

[108] Ibid, 407-409.

Anatole France: The Revolt of the Angels

Anatole France (1844-1924) was a celebrated French author. He became a member of the Académie française in 1896 and was awarded the Nobel Prize in Literature in 1921. In 1922, all of his works were put on the Prohibited Book Index of the Catholic Church, which only served to spark a dramatic increase in demand for his books.

France's satiric novel *The Revolt of the Angels* (1914) is a curious composition. It is a work of Romantic Satanism written half a century after the decline of Romanticism by a man known for his works in the genre of 18th century Classicism. It was France's last novel, written when he was 70. And it is the only work in this primer that uses almost all of our themes of Romantic Satanism. Let's take a closer look.

Books start mysteriously disappearing from the private library of the wealthy d'Esparvieu manor. Maurice d'Esparvieu discovers that the culprit is his own guardian angel, Arcade, who has "devoured the works of theologians, philosophers, physicists, geologists, and naturalists" and has lost his faith:

> *I believe in Him, since my existence depends on His, and if He should fail to exist, I myself should fall into nothingness. I believe in Him, even as the Satyrs and the Mænads believed in Dionysus and for the same reason. I believe in the God of the Jews and the Christians. But I deny that He created the world; at the most He organised but an inferior part of it, and all that He touched bears the mark of His rough and unforeseeing touch. I do not think He is either eternal or infinite, for it is absurd to conceive of a being who is not bounded by space or time. I think Him limited, even very limited. I no longer believe Him to be the only God. For a long time He did not believe it Himself; in the beginning He was a polytheist; later, His pride and the flattery of His worshippers*

made Him a monotheist. His ideas have little connection; He is less powerful than He is thought to be. And, to speak candidly, He is not so much a god as a vain and ignorant demiurge. Those who, like myself, know His true nature, call Him Ialdabaoth.[109]

Ialdabaoth is the Gnostic name of the malevolent demiurge that created the world. France uses Gnosticism to create a critical **reinterpretation** of Christian mythology as well as an **inversion** of good and evil.

The atheistic angel Arcade decides to organize the rebel angels and overthrow Ialdabaoth, invoking the theme of **revolution.** He reveals that there are a number of fallen angels secretly living among humanity. France **normalizes** the former celestials by giving them human characteristics; they work, eat and drink, and fall in love. And unlike their counterparts in Heaven, the fallen angels educate themselves and learn new things about the world around them. Arcade believes knowledge and science will give them an edge in the next conflict with Ialdabaoth:

Nevertheless... man has created science. The important thing is to introduce it into Heaven. When the angels possess some notions of physics, chemistry, astronomy, and physiology; when the study of matter shows them worlds in an atom, and an atom in the myriads of planets; when they see themselves lost between these two infinities; when they weigh and measure the stars, analyse their composition, and calculate their orbits, they will recognise that these monsters work in obedience to forces which no intelligence can define, or that each star has its particular divinity, or indigenous god; and they will realise that the gods of Aldebaran, Betelgeuse,

---

[109] Anatole France, *The Revolt of the Angels,* trans. Wilfrid Jackson (New York, Dodd, Mead and Co., 1922), 37, Kindle.

and Sirius are greater than Ialdabaoth. When at length they come to scrutinise with care the little world in which their lot is cast, and, piercing the crust of the earth, note the gradual evolution of its flora and fauna and the rude origin of man, who, under the shelter of rocks and in cave dwellings, had no God but himself; when they discover that, united by the bonds of universal kinship to plants, beasts, and men, they have successively indued all forms of organic life, from the simplest and the most primitive, until they became at length the most beautiful of the children of light, they will perceive that Ialdabaoth, the obscure demon of an insignificant world lost in space, is imposing on their credulity when he pretends that they issued from nothingness at his bidding; they will perceive that he lies in calling himself the Infinite, the Eternal, the Almighty, and that, so far from having created worlds, he knows neither their number nor their laws. They will perceive that he is like unto one of them; they will despise him, and, shaking off his tyranny, will fling him into the Gehenna where he has hurled those more worthy than himself.[110]

As proof, Arcade observes that science has already diminished the power of the Church:

You deny science has given the Church its death-blow? Is it possible? The Church, at any rate, judges otherwise. Science, which you believe has no power over her, is redoubtable to her, since she proscribes it. From Galileo's dialogues to Monsieur Aulard's little manuals she has condemned all its discoveries. And not without reason.

In former days, when she gathered within her fold all that was

---

[110] France, *Revolt of the Angels*, 47.

*great in human thought, the Church held sway over the bodies as
well as over the souls of men, and imposed unity of obedience by
fire and sword. To-day her power is but a shadow and the elect
among the great minds have withdrawn from her. That is the state
to which Science has reduced her.*[111]

When Arcade and his comrades meet the ancient angel Nectaire, he
gives a firsthand account of the original war in Heaven that led to
Satan's downfall. France's **reinterpretation** of this myth is much more
favorable to Satan.

The war in Heaven starts because Lucifer is more attractive and
virtuous than Ialdabaoth:

*He was the most beautiful of all the Seraphim. He shone with
intelligence and daring. His great heart was big with all the virtues
born of pride: frankness, courage, constancy in trial, indomitable
hope.*[112]

Furthermore, Lucifer preferred to hang out with rebels like himself:

*Lucifer, who held vile things in proud disdain, despised this rabble
of commonplace spirits for ever wallowing in a life of feasts and
pleasure. But to those who were possessed of a daring spirit, a
restless soul, to those fired with a wild love of liberty, he proffered
friendship, which was returned with adoration. These latter
deserted in a mass the mountain of God and yielded to the Seraph
the homage which That Other would fain have kept for himself*

---

[111] Ibid, 48.

[112] Ibid, 68.

alone.[113]

Ialdabaoth gets jealous and the war in Heaven begins. Lucifer and the rebel angels put up a valiant fight and defeat Ialdabaoth's armies, but when they attempt to scale the mountain of God, Ialdabaoth repulses them with his thunderbolts and they fall from Heaven, defeated.

Nectaire's description of Hell is reminiscent of Milton:

> *I awoke in a darkness filled with lamentations. And when my eyes had grown accustomed to the dense shadows I saw round me my companions in arms, scattered in thousands on the sulphurous ground, lit by fitful gleams of livid light. My eyes perceived but fields of lava, smoking craters, and poisonous swamps.*
>
> *Mountains of ice and shadowy seas shut in the horizon. A brazen sky hung heavy on our brows. And the horror of the place was such that we wept as we sat, crouched elbow on knee, our cheeks resting on our clenched hands.*
>
> *But soon, raising my eyes, I beheld the Seraph standing before me like a tower.*[114] *Over his pristine splendour sorrow had cast its mantle of sombre majesty.*
>
> *"Comrades," said he, "we must be happy and rejoice, for behold we are delivered from celestial servitude. Here we are free, and it were better to be free in Hell than serve in Heaven.*[115] *We are not conquered, since the will to conquer is still ours. We have caused the Throne of the jealous God to totter; by our hands it shall fall.*

---

[113] Ibid, 69.

[114] Compare with Milton, *Paradise Lost,* Book 1, lines 590-591: "In shape and gesture proudly eminent/Stood like a Towr;"

[115] Compare with Milton, *Paradise Lost,* Book 1, line 263: "Better to reign in Hell, then serve in Heav'n."

Arise, therefore, and be of good heart."[116]

They make one more attempt to attack the palace of Ialdabaoth but are repelled by thunderbolts and lightning and fall once again. Satan refuses to admit defeat:

> *"Friends," he said, "if victory is denied us now, it is because we are neither worthy nor capable of victory. Let us determine wherein we have failed. Nature shall not be ruled, the sceptre of the Universe shall not be grasped, Godhead shall not be won, save by knowledge alone. We must conquer the thunder; to that task we must apply ourselves unwearyingly. It is not blind courage (no one this day has shown more courage than have you) which will win us the courts of Heaven; but rather study and reflection. In these silent realms where we are fallen, let us meditate, seeking the hidden causes of things; let us observe the course of Nature; let us pursue her with compelling ardour and all-conquering desire; let us strive to penetrate her infinite grandeur, her infinite minuteness. Let us seek to know when she is barren and when she brings forth fruit; how she makes cold and heat, joy and sorrow, life and death; how she assembles and disperses her elements, how she produces both the light air we breathe and the rocks of diamond and sapphire whence we have been precipitated, the divine fire wherewith we have been scarred and the soaring thought which stirs our minds."*[117]

Satan and the fallen angels turn their attention to the newly-created earth and find themselves fascinated with humanity, whose "miserable lot and his painstaking spirit aroused the sympathy of the vanquished

---

[116] France, *Revolt of the Angels,* 71.

[117] Ibid.

angels, who discerned in him an audacity equaling their own, and the germ of pride that was at once their glory and their bane."[118] The fallen angels teach man the secrets of fire, agriculture, and other elements of civilization. It is revealed that the fallen angels have played a significant role in shaping human history, that Satan and his minions have become the benefactors and protectors of humanity since the beginning of mortal time, and that some of them have even been worshiped as gods of Egypt and Greece. Civilization flourishes under their guidance.

Life seems pretty good until Ialdabaoth (aka Iahveh) decides to get involved. France's **reinterpretation** of Christian theology through Nectaire is scathing:

Of all the spirits, Iahveh appeared the least prepared for victory. His ignorance, his cruelty, his ostentation, his Asiatic luxury, his disdain of laws, his affectation of rendering himself invisible, all these things were calculated to offend those Greeks and Latins who had absorbed the teaching of Dionysus and the Muses. He himself felt he was incapable of winning the allegiance of free men and of cultivated minds, and he employed cunning. To seduce their souls he invented a fable which, although not so ingenious as the myths wherewith we have surrounded the spirits of our disciples of old, could, nevertheless, influence those feebler intellects which are to be found everywhere in great masses. He declared that men having committed a crime against him, an hereditary crime, should pay the penalty for it in their present life and in the life to come (for mortals vainly imagine that their existence is prolonged in hell); and the astute Iahveh gave out that he had sent his own son to earth to redeem with his blood the debt of mankind. It is not credible that a penalty should redress a fault, and it is still less credible that the innocent should pay for the guilty. The sufferings of the innocent atone for nothing, and do but add one evil to another. Nevertheless, unhappy creatures were found to adore Iahveh and his son, the expiator, and to announce their mysteries as good tidings. We should not be surprised at this folly. Have we not seen many times indeed human beings who, poor and naked, prostrate themselves before all the phantoms of fear, and rather than follow the teaching of well-disposed demons, obey the commandments of cruel demiurges?[119]

Nectaire recasts history as a struggle between the benevolent fallen angels and the evil minions of Ialdabaoth. The rise of Christianity brings all kinds of evils to mankind: war and oppression, suffering and death, ignorance and hatred. Then, starting with the Renaissance, humanity is inspired "with an ardent desire to love and to know" by renewed interest in the "antique world" of the Greeks and Romans, and Christianity starts to go into decline.[120] This decline is temporarily reversed by Martin Luther, "a German monk, all swollen with beer and theology," who "repaired, calked, and refloated the damaged ship of the Church."[121] This leads to a "time of great terror when Papists and Reformers rivalled one another in violence and cruelty."[122] Christianity's decline continues with the Enlightenment, when "the spirit of research was developed, reverence was lost; the pride of the flesh was diminished and the mind acquired fresh energy."[123] Nectaire's story ends with an account of the French Revolution, the rise of Napoleon, and a condemnation of war:

---

[119] Ibid, 77-78.

[120] Ibid, 83.

[121] Ibid, 84.

[122] Ibid, 85.

[123] Ibid, 86.

They did not understand that war, which trained the courage and founded the cities of barbarous and ignorant men, brings to the victor himself but ruin and misery, and is nothing but a horrible and stupid crime when nations are united together by common bonds of art, science, and trade.[124]

Arcade convinces Nectaire to join the revolt. The fallen angels gather, declare war on Heaven, and prepare for battle. At the end of the novel, Arcade and his friends finally meet Satan and ask him to lead the revolt of the angels. Satan invites them to rest and refresh themselves, stating that he will give them an answer in the morning.

That night Satan has a vivid dream about the war in Heaven. After three days of battle, the fallen angels devastate the celestial hosts; then they bombard the palace of Ialdabaoth upon the Holy Mountain with explosive "electrophores" (weapons of science), forcing God to flee.

Then the dream turns sour:

And Satan had himself crowned God. Thronging round the glittering walls of Heavenly Jerusalem, apostles, pontiffs, virgins, martyrs, confessors, the whole company of the elect, who during the fierce battle had enjoyed delightful tranquility, tasted infinite joy in the spectacle of the coronation.

The elect saw with ravishment the Most High precipitated into Hell, and Satan seated on the throne of the Lord. In conformity with the will of God which had cut them off from sorrow they sang in the ancient fashion the praises of their new Master.

And Satan, piercing space with his keen glance, contemplated the little globe of earth and water where of old he had planted the vine and formed the first tragic chorus. And he fixed his gaze on that

---

[124] Ibid, 88.

Rome where the fallen God had founded his empire on fraud and lie. Nevertheless, at that moment a saint ruled over the Church. Satan saw him praying and weeping. And he said to him:

"To thee I entrust my Spouse. Watch over her faithfully. In thee I confirm the right and power to decide matters of doctrine, to regulate the use of the sacraments, to make laws and to uphold purity of morals. And the faithful shall be under obligation to conform thereto. My Church is eternal, and the gates of hell shall not prevail against it. Thou art infallible. Nothing is changed."

And the successor of the apostles felt flooded with rapture. He prostrated himself, and with his forehead touching the floor, replied:

"O Lord, my God, I recognise Thy voice! Thy breath has been wafted like balm to my heart. Blessed be Thy name. Thy will be done on Earth, as it is in Heaven. Lead us not into temptation, but deliver us from evil."

And Satan found pleasure in praise and in the exercise of his grace; he loved to hear his wisdom and his power belauded. He listened with joy to the canticles of the cherubim who celebrated his good deeds, and he took no pleasure in listening to Nectaire's flute, because it celebrated nature's self, yielded to the insect and to the blade of grass their share of power and love, and counselled happiness and freedom. Satan, whose flesh had crept, in days gone by, at the idea that suffering prevailed in the world, now felt himself inaccessible to pity. He regarded suffering and death as the happy results of omnipotence and sovereign kindness. And the savour of the blood of victims rose upward towards him like sweet incense. He fell to condemning intelligence and to hating curiosity. He himself refused to learn anything more, for fear that in acquiring fresh knowledge he might let it be seen that he had not known everything at the very outset. He took pleasure in mystery, and believing that he would seem less great by being understood, he affected to be unintelligible. Dense fumes of Theology filled his brain. One day, following the example of his predecessor, he conceived the notion of proclaiming himself one god in three persons. Seeing Arcade smile as this proclamation was made, he drove him from his presence. Istar and Zita had long since returned to earth. Thus centuries passed like seconds. Now, one day, from the altitude of his throne, he plunged his gaze into the depths of the pit and saw Ialdabaoth in the Gehenna where he himself had long lain enchained. Amid the everlasting gloom Ialdabaoth still retained his lofty mien. Blackened and shattered, terrible and sublime, he glanced upwards at the palace of the King of Heaven with a look of proud disdain, then turned away his head. And the new god, as he looked upon his foe, beheld the light of intelligence and love pass across his sorrow-stricken countenance. And lo! Ialdabaoth was now contemplating the Earth and, seeing it sunk in wickedness and suffering, he began to foster thoughts of kindliness in his heart. On a sudden he rose up, and beating the ether with his mighty arms, as though with oars, he hastened thither to instruct and to console mankind. Already his vast shadow shed upon the unhappy planet a shade soft as a night of love.

And Satan awoke bathed in an icy sweat.

Nectaire, Istar, Arcade, and Zita were standing round him. The finches were singing.

"Comrades," said the great archangel, "no—we will not conquer the heavens. Enough to have the power. War engenders war, and victory defeat. God, conquered, will become Satan; Satan, conquering, will become God. May the fates spare me this terrible lot; I love the Hell which formed my genius. I love the Earth where I have done some good, if it be possible to do any good in this fearful world where beings live but by rapine. Now, thanks to us, the god of old is dispossessed of his terrestrial empire, and every

thinking being on this globe disdains him or knows him not. But what matter that men should be no longer submissive to Ialdabaoth if the spirit of Ialdabaoth is still in them; if they, like him, are jealous, violent, quarrelsome, and greedy, and the foes of the arts and of beauty? What matter that they have rejected the ferocious Demiurge, if they do not hearken to the friendly demons who teach all truths; to Dionysus, Apollo, and the Muses? As to ourselves, celestial spirits, sublime demons, we have destroyed Ialdabaoth, our Tyrant, if in ourselves we have destroyed Ignorance and Fear."

And Satan, turning to the gardener, said:

"Nectaire, you fought with me before the birth of the world. We were conquered because we failed to understand that Victory is a Spirit, and that it is in ourselves and in ourselves alone that we must attack and destroy Ialdabaoth."[125]

Satan does not want to become Ialdabaoth; instead he encourages his comrades to destroy the spirit of Ialdabaoth within themselves, to defeat the tyrant of ignorance and fear.

That the angels do not go to war in the end is significant. France published *Revolt of the Angels* in 1914, just as World War I was getting started, and the novel contains many condemnations of war and the death and destruction it causes.

---

[125] Ibid, 141-142.

Conclusion

Romantic Satanism had been connected in many ways with the Age of Revolution, and when that age ended, the genre went into decline. In the 1840's Romanticism started to give way to Realism. Realism rejected the emotional, the exotic, the heroic, and the sublime for realistic portrayals of everyday people and their environment, with a focus on societal changes brought about by industry and commercialization and its impact on the working class. The rise of Occultism in France and England during the last half of the 19th century and its association with Satan and demonic forces fostered more negative perceptions of Satan, as did the Taxil Hoax (1885-1897), which purported that the Freemasons were secretly ruled by an evil Luciferian cabal seeking to destroy the Catholic Church.

The Romantic Satanists were the first Satanic activists. When conservatives and anti-revolutionaries applied Satanic labels to revolutions and their supporters, the Romantic Satanists reinterpreted and updated Satanic mythology to cast their opponents as evil and tyrannical and to promote political reform. They were not religious Satanists, but they used Satan to provoke and scandalize people in order to draw attention to their own political activism. Some of the Romantic Satanists were even fined, imprisoned, and exiled for their political views.

The rise of Evangelical Christianity in the 21st century has brought new challenges to our liberty and equality. American Evangelicals seek to impose their sadistic and oppressive religion upon a country where more people than ever are rejecting Christianity, repulsed by judgmental and hypocritical Christians and sickened by an epidemic of child abuse within their churches. Evangelicals seek to destroy religious pluralism, deny rights to LBGTQ+ folks and people of color, and subjugate women. They are threats to our freedom and traitors to this country that must be stopped.

Unlike many modern Christians, Evangelicals still believe in Satan as a supernatural entity at war with God. By engaging in Satanic activism, we take on the role of their spiritual enemies. We threaten Evangelicals when we force national and local governments to uphold religious pluralism, and when we advocate for equal rights for all people regardless of their race, gender, religion, or sexual orientation. Like the Romantic Satanists before us, Satanic activists have cast Satan as the rebel and liberator fighting against the tyranny and oppression of the Evangelical menace.

Like the Romantic Satan, we must rise up and fight. Now is the time to act. Now, more than ever, we must "Awake, arise, or be for ever fallen."

Glossary

Age of Revolution: the period between 1774 and 1849 during which many revolutions took place, in Europe and around the world.

Anarchism: A political theory holding all forms of governmental authority to be unnecessary and undesirable and advocating a society based on voluntary cooperation and free association of individuals and groups.

Apocryphal: Of or relating to the Apocrypha, various religious writings of uncertain origin regarded by some as inspired, but rejected by most authorities.

Canto: One of the major divisions of a long poem.

Deism: A movement or system of thought advocating natural religion, emphasizing morality, and in the 18th century denying the interference of the Creator with the laws of the universe.

Deconstruction: The analytic examination of something (such as a theory) often in order to reveal its inadequacy.

Demiurge: A Gnostic subordinate deity who is the creator of the material world.

Epic: A long narrative poem in elevated style recounting the deeds of a legendary or historical hero, such as Homer's *Iliad*.

Gehenna: A valley outside of Jerusalem where idolatrous Jews sacrificed their children to Moloch. Later it became the town dump, filled with garbage, sewage, and dead bodies. To get rid of the garbage and the awful smell that came with it, they set it on fire. There was a constant flow of garbage being dumped in the valley, so the fires seemed to burn eternally, and thus Gehenna became synonymous with Hell.

Millenarian: Related to the idea that the second coming of Jesus will establish a thousand years of peace and happiness upon the Earth.

Pentateuch: The Jewish name for the first five books of the Old Testament.

Satanism: The veneration or adoration of Satan as a metaphor, archetype, supernatural force, and/or deity.

Sedition: Incitement of resistance to or insurrection against lawful authority.

Utilitarianism: A theory that the aim of action should be the largest possible balance of pleasure over pain or the greatest happiness of the greatest number.

Bibliography

All websites accessed 1/18/20.

Baudelaire, Charles. "Litany to Satan." Translated by James Elroy Flecker. In *The Collected Poems of James Elroy Flecker*. New York: Doubleday, Page & Co, 1916. https://en.wikisource.org/wiki/The_collected_poems_of_James_Elroy_Flecker/Litany_to_Satan.

Blake, William. *The Poetical Works of William Blake*. Edited by John Sampson. New York: Oxford University Press, 1908. https://www.bartleby.com/235 /253.html.

—. *William Blake: The Complete Illuminated Books*. New York: Thames & Hudson, 2000.

Lord Byron. *Cain, A Mystery*. Edited by Peter Cochran. PDF. http: //newsteadabbeybyronsociety.org/works/poems.htm.

—. *Don Juan*. https://www.poetryfoundation.org/poems/43828/ don-juan-dedication.

—. *Manfred*. In Charles W. Eliot, Ed., *The Harvard Classics*, Vol. XVIII, Part 6. New York: P.F. Collier & Son, 1914 https://www.bartleby.com/br /01806.html.

—. *A Vision of Judgment*. Edited by Peter Cochran. PDF. https://peter-cochran .files.wordpress.com/2009/03/the_vision_of_judgement3.pdf

Constant, Alphonse Louis (Eliphas Levi). *The Bible of Liberty*. Daath Gnosis Publishing, 2012.

Dyrendal, Asbjørn, James R. Lewis, and Jesper AA. Petersen. *The Invention of Satanism*. New York: Oxford University Press, 2016.

Faxneld, Per. *Satanic Feminism: Lucifer as the Liberator of Woman in Nineteenth-Century Culture.* New York: Oxford University Press, 2017.

Faxneld, Per and Jesper Aa. Petersen, eds. *The Devil's Party: Satanism in Modernity.* New York: Oxford University Press, 2013.

Flowers, Stephen E. *Lords of the Left-Hand Path.* Rochester: Inner Traditions, 2012.

France, Anatole. *The Revolt of the Angels.* Translated by Wilfrid Jackson. New York: Dodd, Mead and Co., 1922. Kindle.

Godwin, William. *An Enquiry into Political Justice, and its Influence on General Virtue and Happiness.* Vol.1. London: G.G.J. and J. Robinson, 1793. https://oll.libertyfund.org/titles/godwin-an-enquiry-concerning-political-justice-vol-i.

Greenblatt, Stephen, et al., eds. *The Norton Anthology of English Literature*, 9th ed., Vol D. New York: W.W. Norton & Company, 2012.

Hugo, Victor. *God and The End of Satan.* Translated by R.G. Skinner. Chicago: Swan Isle Press, 2014.

Levi, Eliphas. *Dogma and Ritual of High Magic.* Translated by John Michael Greer and Mark Anthony Mikituk. New York: TarcherPerigee, 2017.

Lujik, Ruben van. *Children of Lucifer: The Origins of Modern Religious Satanism.* New York: Oxford University Press, 2016.

Milton, John. *Paradise Lost.* Thomas H. Luxon, General Editor. Trustees of Dartmouth College, 2020. https://www.dartmouth.edu/~milton /reading_room/pl/book_1/text.shtml.

The New American Bible, Revised Edition. 2011. http://usccb.org/bible/index.cfm.

Paine, Thomas. *Age of Reason.* 1796. https://web.archive.org/web /20050306021320/http://www.ushistory.org/paine/reason/index.htm.

Proudhon, Pierre Joseph. *On Justice in Revolution and Church.* Translated by Shawn P. Wilbur (2018). https://www.libertarian-labyrinth.org/working-translations /proudhon-justice-eighth-study/.

—. *The System of Economic Contradictions*. Translated by Benjamin R. Tucker. (1888). https://theanarchistlibrary.org/library/pierre- joseph-proudhon-system-of-economical-contradictions-or-the-philosophy-of-poverty.

Rapport, Michael. *Nineteenth-Century Europe*. Houndmills, UK: Palgrave Macmillan, 2005.

Schock, Peter A. *Romantic Satanism: Myth and the Historical Movement in Blake, Shelley, and Byron*. Houndmills, UK: Palgrave Macmillan, 2003.

Shelley, Percy Bysshe. "A Defense of Poetry." 2009. https://www.poetryfoundation.org/articles/69388/a-defence-of-poetry.

—. *The Devil's Walk*. 2013. https://en.wikisource.org/wiki/The_Devil%27s_Walk_(Shelley).

—. "On the Devil and Devils." In *The Prose Works of Percy Bysshe Shelley*. Edited by Harry Buxton Forman. London: Reeves and Turner, 1880. https://en.wikisource.org/wiki/The_Prose_Works_of_Percy_Bysshe_Shelley/On_the_Devil,_and_Devils.

—. *Prometheus Unbound*. London: C and J Ollier, 1820. http://knarf.english. upenn.edu/PShelley/promtp.html.

—. *Queen Mab*. London: W. Clark, 1821. https://en.wikisource.org/wiki /Queen_Mab/Notes.

—. *The Revolt of Islam*. 2019. https://en.wikisource.org/wiki/The_Revolt_of_Islam.

Southey, Robert. *A Vision of Judgement*. PDF. In Appendix to Lord Byron. *A Vision of Judgment*, Edited by Peter Cochran. https://petercochran.files.wordpress.com/2009/03/the_vision_of_judgement3.pdf.

Tristan, Flora. *The Emancipation of Woman*. Translated by Kirk Watson. Kindle.

Vigny, Alfred de. *Eloa, or the Sister of the Angels*. Translated by Alan de Corré. https://minds.wisconsin.edu/bitstream/handle/1793/61400/eloaweb

.html?sequence=1.

Voltaire. *The Philosophical Dictionary.* Edited by H.I. Woolf. New York Knopf, 1924. https://history.hanover.edu/texts/voltaire/volindex. htm.

Wikipedia. *The Vision of Judgment.* 2020. https://en.wikipedia.org/ wiki/The_Vision_of_Judgment#cite_note-1.

Index

Made in the USA
Monee, IL
02 December 2023

47254857R00077